PREPARING FOR REVIVAL

To Margaret

Make room for the King
of Glory. He's coming!

[signature]

Preparing
for
Revival

BRIAN MILLS

STL Books
Bromley, Kent

KINGSWAY PUBLICATIONS
EASTBOURNE

Biblical quotations are from the
New International Version © 1973, 1978, 1984 by the
International Bible Society. Anglicisation © 1979, 1984
by Hodder & Stoughton
Use is also made of the Authorised Version, Crown Copyright,
and The Living Bible © Tyndale House Publishers 1971.

Front cover photo: Art Directors Photolibrary – London

British Library Cataloguing in Publication Data

Mills, Brian
Preparing for revival.
1. Christian Church. Revivals
I. Title
269.24

ISBN 0–86065–505–9 (Kingsway)
1–85078–070–6 (STL)

STL Books are published by Send The Light
(Operation Mobilisation), PO Box 48, Bromley, Kent, England.

Printed in Great Britain for
KINGSWAY PUBLICATIONS LTD
1 St Anne's Road, Eastbourne, E Sussex BN21 3UN by
Courier International Ltd, Tiptree, Essex.
Typeset by J&L Composition Ltd., Filey, North Yorkshire.

Contents

Foreword   7
Introduction   9
Acknowledgements   11
Section I : What is Revival?
  1. Breath of God   15
  2. What is Revival?   21
  3. Doubts and Disagreements   31
  4. God of Surprises   43
Section II : Features of Revival
  5. The Presence of God   55
  6. The Holiness of God   67
  7. Awareness of Sin   85
  8. Come Back, Go, Convert and Sing   97
  9. Let My People Pray   109
 10. Spiritual Warfare   127
 11. Know Your Lord, Know Your Enemy   141
 12. Combating Demonic Forces   155
 13. Highway Through the Heavenlies   169
Section III : Who Wants Revival?
 14. Who Wants Revival?   187
 15. Preparing for Revival   197
 16. A Vision for Revival   211
Appendix: A Call to Prayer   221

Foreword

The title of this book, *Preparing for Revival*, strikes an immediate note of expectancy—an expectancy that we are going to witness an outpouring of the Holy Spirit in our country before very long. A spiritual 'awakening' lies ahead of us which will see the church in Britain involved in gathering a great harvest for God. That is the hope and longing of the author.

There have always been people who kept a vision for revival before tham. Brian Mills is such a person. If the interest is now widening, then not a little of that is due to his own great efforts over many years to encourage Christian people to pray for revival.

This book is a continuation of that dedicated ministry. He draws on a large store of pertinent and interesting episodes from revivals both past and present—like a great many others he has held on to the vision of revival, and been constantly stirred by the great things God has done as he has poured out his Spirit. As he expresses his enthusiasm and excitement, he inspires us with an eager desire to see the holiness and majesty of God revealed both inside and outside of the church.

This book, as those who know Brian Mills well would

expect, becomes most expansive and earnest when addressing the subject of praying for revival. Most people will readily acknowledge the fact that revival demands earnest prayer, but often it is with a nod of assent rather than positive action. What comes out of the pages of this book, however, is an impression of personal commitment from someone who not only knows the facts, but who also has a burning determination to pray and get others to pray with him. Allied to that determination is a practical outlook which helps to move exhortation into activity.

Not least among the aspects of praying for revival is spiritual warfare. Revival is a time of great defeat for the Enemy. It is a time when he is stripped of many of his holds on humanity. Brian Mills points out that the call to prolonged and earnest prayer has far less to do with moving God's heart to bless than with moving the obstacles which Satan puts in the way of God's intended blessing. We need to understand this battle, particularly the pivotal place of prayer for its successful outcome. One suspects that those who have prayed for revival in past years have been conscious of the forces which oppose the Spirit, even though the literature about revival does not often reveal the nature of the prayers that were made. It is good, therefore, to have this aspect of revival praying placed clearly before us. It may well be that our own generation needs it more than previous generations.

Sometimes I am afraid that the word 'revival' will become an 'in' word, yet one more piece of jargon in the Christian vocabulary. That must be avoided at all costs. I have no doubt that the spirit which informs this book will do much to counter that danger.

BOB DUNNETT
Vice Principal,
Birmingham Bible Institute

Introduction

I've just completed an eighteen-hour flight from London to the Far East. The plane took us over many countries and oceans. We had three changes of crew. We became almost 'one' with our seats. Being in a kind of time-warp, we lost track of time and location. We knew our destination, but in between we could have been anywhere. The interior of the plane became our home, except for welcome breaks in airport transit lounges, which took us out of our cocooned environment into a semblance of 'normal' civilisation. At the end of the journey the one thing we all needed was to be revived!

It's a bit like that with us and the church. Most of us are passive passengers on the journey of a lifetime where our destination is known. Our active crew (ie church leaders) may change. Our in-flight meals may vary, but in between life goes on hour by hour, day by day, year by year. We become cocooned in our spiritual time-warps, oblivious to what's going on in the real world around us. What do we need? Revival!

In this book I've attempted to define revival, describe its variety, identify its characteristics and outline the requirements for us if we are ever going to experience such reviving. I believe God wants to bring such times to his church. He realises we need his power that demonstrates his greatness for all the world to see. He also knows that our human weaknesses need to be overwhelmed by his divine strength; our boredom with the glory of a God who still reveals himself; our mundanity with the infinite variety of his working in his world.

In short, I believe God wants to bring a spiritual awakening to his church of whatever nation. But, paradoxically he seems to wait for his people to capture the vision, and catch the burden for it in such a way that it leads to extraordinary prayer and seeking after God. He wants us to co-operate with him, to work through us and to give us the joy of seeing his glory come down.

I have to confess that I have not until now witnessed at first hand a general spiritual awakening that affected whole communities. As I write I'm on my way to 'revival areas' to experience for myself what God is doing. Maybe there will be a sequel! However we can all learn what is involved by examining what God has done in the past and is doing in the world today.

My prayer is that the reality of what God can do will lead you into urgent and specific prayer. I hope readers will be neither intimidated nor alienated by what they read. Rather that God's convicting power and presence will come on them, leading them to 'humble themselves and pray, and seek his face and turn from their wicked ways'.

Brian Mills

Acknowledgements

My thanks are due to the following who helped me bring a burden to fruition.

The late Dr Edwin Orr for his knowledge of revival and his encouragement of me personally in pursuing the vision for it.

Linda Rose and Gill Bacon for their typing and retyping of the original manuscript (thank God for word processors!).

Maggie Fielden for proof-reading, checking quotations, etc.

David Porter who reworked some of the manuscript.

To you for buying it!

Section I
What is Revival?

I

Breath of God

Revival is God-breathed. It is him at work in an awesome way.

Here are some pen-pictures:

I had been preaching about the work of God in revival, both in history and in individual lives. The congregation wanted to know more, so I stayed behind for questions. But it was not long before the questions stopped, and those who had been asking them began to confess sins and wrong attitudes, and to pray for individuals with whom they had difficult relationships. Praise and worship followed; we joined hands and sang 'Bind us together', and our hands remained joined for fifteen to twenty minutes as God worked among us. Three times I pronounced a final blessing. God had other ideas. When the meeting was finally declared over, it had been in progress for four-and-a-quarter hours, and counselling went on afterwards until the early hours of the morning.

*   *   *

We had been watching a Christian film at our seaside house party, and were putting the equipment away. One of our workers was on the beach, where she had been praying.

Suddenly, she saw a human form coming from the sea. It passed by her and went on into the house. At that precise moment, the whole party experienced the supernatural power of God, and every person who was not already a Christian was immediately born again.

*   *   *

I'd been preaching some solid doctrine from Romans. We stayed on in the marquee for a time of prayer. It was a still summer evening. Suddenly, while we were praying, the canvas began to flap. 'It is the Holy Spirit,' said the person next to me. And so it was; like a wind, the breath of God moved through the camp and all but one person met with God that night.

*   *   *

They were all one-off events. They all happened in Britain during the 1980s. No doubt there were many more that others could tell of. Do they constitute revival? No, but they are supernatural- or extraordinary- manifestations. They illustrate that God is still working in ways that take us by surprise. They leave me awe-struck and wanting more, and they whetted the appetite of those Christian leaders who were present.

The work of God in revival is not limited by time or by geography.

Duncan Campbell was asked to address a congregation at the church. He preached briefly, they sang, and then he went outside. As Campbell stood waiting to be taken for his meal a man inside the building was heard to pray. 'Lord, you dare not fail us, you must not fail us . . . . Have you not promised: "I will pour water on him that is thirsty and floods upon the dry ground"? Lord, your honour is at stake.' Everyone stood still and, by this time, the congregation had increased to six or seven hundred. They sang the Psalm, 'When the Lord turned again the captivity of Zion' and then all squashed into the church again. Campbell was wedged into the pulpit with several other people and began to preach. Within ten minutes he could not be heard above the cries of penitent people. People were so deeply convicted of their sinfulness that some came close to despair. One burly farmer cried out, 'Oh God, I feel that hell itself would be too good for me.' Men and women were in distress as the awfulness of sin dawned on them. Prayer continued throughout the night and, at 4 am the next day, Campbell prepared to leave the church to go to the manse for supper! Before he could do so however, a messenger came to tell him that a large crowd had gathered by the police station, waiting to be addressed by him. As the preacher went on foot from the parish church to the police constable's house, he saw grown men kneeling by the roadside and a group of women by a haystack crying to God for mercy. Without advertising, God had begun to grip the community of the outer Hebrides.[1]

Shortly before his death, Len Moules wrote:

> One could almost use the term an 'epidemic' of revivals. It is difficult to keep abreast of the reports of the local stirrings of God and spiritual awakenings that are becoming nationwide in several countries. In war-torn Ethiopia there were glorious reports of tremendous awakenings in the mountains of South-West Ethiopia, with results that rank with some of the greatest conversion movements in Africa's history.[2]

In Uganda, in the pre-Amin era, three Christian girls at a boarding school took part in a riot. Their testimony as Christians was destroyed as a result. When they realised this they were so convicted about what they had done that instead of going to a disco as they had planned, they went to the school chapel to confess their sins to God. Two members of staff joined them there. Gradually, other girls arrived. Four hours later, 400 girls were calling on the name of the Lord and confessing their need of forgiveness. All in the school became Christians. They then set about sharing their faith with the people in the nearby community. Once they were all converted, they asked to be sent out to the surrounding villages to preach the gospel.

In central Cuba, a miraculous healing took place at a 150-seat chapel at the beginning of a nine-day mission. The repercussions were so astounding that at one time 5,000 people crowded into the chapel. During those nine days, 1,200 people became Christians, and there were further healings. The two pastors were put in prison, but Cuban believers commented, 'Although the authorities stopped this crusade, they cannot stop the Holy Spirit.' Revival spread to the rest of Cuba.

There are numerous examples like the ones I have described.

Every outpouring of the Spirit, every supernatural manifestation, every divine intervention, is an expression of the many-faceted nature of God. He is holy, without sin; he wants to glorify himself on earth. He wants all men to come to a knowledge of the truth. He wants reality, honesty and holiness among his people. He acts according to his mighty power.

> In many separate revelations and in different ways God spoke of old to our forefathers in and by the prophets. But now in the last of these days he has spoken to us through and in the person of his Son. God's Son shines out with God's glory—he is the perfect imprint and very image of God's nature, upholding and maintaining and guiding and propelling the universe by his mighty word of power. When he had by offering himself accomplished our cleansing of sin and riddance of guilt, he sat down at the right hand of the divine Majesty on high (Heb 1:1-3, paraphrased from the Amplified Bible).

This to me is a complete summary of the work of God in revival. It is personified in his Son Jesus Christ as the instrument. It is set in the context of history as part of

God's on-going purposes. It reveals that revival is the
sovereign work of God.

Within revival there is the awesome paradoxical fusion
of the revelation of the glory of God in the world, with
the revelation of man's depravity and need of total
cleansing. God speaks *into* the human situation as well as
to it. He reveals his power. He begins to remake us in his
own image, so that humanity can enjoy what in the
beginning was forfeited by disobedience— communion
with God.

God is glorifying himself among us on earth, so that
we may be glorified with him in the eternal presence of
his majestic being in heaven. In that perspective, the
overwhelming sense of the presence of God which is
experienced in revivals is a mere foretaste of that future
presence which will last for ever.

> O breath of God come sweeping through us,
> Revive thy church with life and power.
> O breath of Life, come, cleanse, renew us,
> And fit thy church to meet this hour.
>
> (*Bessie P. Head*)

Notes

1. Redemption Magazine, (November 1985).
2. Clifford Wadey (ed.), Spiritual Revival (Walters, 1982), pp 15–16.

2
What is Revival?

If you ask most Christians what they understand by the word 'revival', they will tell you that revival means 'God working in an extraordinary way'.

When stories are told of past and present revivals, the emphasis is often placed on the supernatural and spectacular events that accompanied them. In such times, we are told, God's power and his presence were poured out abundantly; things happened which you do not normally find in 'everyday' Christianity.

So when something out of the ordinary happens in *our* Christian lives and churches, our tendency—and it's a very human one—is to say: 'It is unusual, it is extraordinary; it must be revival! Or at least a *touch* of revival.'

I have read many stories of revival, and I've heard some first hand from people who were involved. Quite clearly, revivals are accompanied by the presence of extraordinary and spectacular events. But I want to suggest that there is much, much more to revival than that.

Indeed, I am inclined to believe that the extraordinary events we read about in revival ought to be part of our *everyday* Christianity! But because we live so much of our

Christianity at a subnormal (sometimes even abnormal) level, we think that such things are out of the ordinary when we do encounter them.

Yet things we might associate only with revival are happening all the time elsewhere, at different times and in different sections of local and national church life.

So what is a revival, over and above extraordinary events?

Hallmarks of revival

When a revival or spiritual awakening happens, spectacular events no longer happen only occasionally. They become everyday occurrences. Also, they are not just witnessed locally by a few people. The news spreads far and wide. The extent and the scope of what God is doing leaves us gasping in awe and wonder. 'This is the Lord's doing,' we cry out, 'and it is marvellous in our eyes!'

When revival happens, everything gathers speed. Evangelism produces increased numbers of conversions, churches grow, new churches are planted. Supernatural acts of God such as healings, which may have happened sporadically before, are suddenly seen in large numbers. The overwhelming sense of the presence of God, which we sometimes experience in large, spiritually- and emotionally-charged meetings, is now experienced by individuals who may have no thought or desire for spiritual things. God's glory comes down!

As people begin to understand clearly the holiness of God, they become acutely sensitive to their own sinfulness. Their guilt becomes an intolerable burden to them. They seek forgiveness, and they find it. The effects on morality, in both Christian and secular circles, are profound. And in times of revival, prayer—which before was restricted to set times and situations—becomes an all-consuming passion.

Defining revival

Many people have attempted to define revival. Most of their definitions contain some truth. But nobody could hope to define in a single statement the entire varied nature of God, as we see it in a heaven-sent revival.

Arthur Wallis called revival 'such a display of God's holiness and power that often human personalities are overshadowed and human programmes abandoned. It is God breaking into the consciousness of men in majesty and glory.'[1]

Dr J Edwin Orr (the evangelist, historian and world authority on spiritual awakenings) said: 'An awakening is a movement of the Holy Spirit bringing about a revival of New Testament Christianity in the Church of Christ and in its related community.' He went on:

> The outpouring of the Spirit effects the reviving of the Church, the awakening of the masses, and the movement of uninstructed peoples towards the Christian faith; the revived Church by many or by few is moved to engage in evangelism, in teaching and in social action. Such an awakening may run its course briefly or it may last a life-time.[2]

Some will say, 'But isn't that happening already? Isn't that what we mean when we talk about church growth?'

It's true, one could point to times when the church has increased dramatically in numbers. But often that has not had the impact on the 'masses and uninstructed' that we might expect after studying the historic revivals.

Revival is a unique work of God. We need to know how to recognise it. We need to know what it is, and that means that we need first to know what it is *not*.

Revival is not renewal

Renewal affects people in the church over a period of time, but it does not affect society. Revival, however, does both. We can regard renewal as part of an overall spiritual awakening, but (as Orr points out) it is only partial, if only the church feels the effects. So, while we praise God for the effect that renewal—charismatic and otherwise—has had on the church in recent years, we still long for all that God has in store for us as his people to be poured out among *all* mankind. We long to see the fulfilment of God's words which Joel quotes in his prophecy: 'I will pour out my Spirit on *all people*.' (Joel 2:28, italics mine).

Revival is not evangelism

In times of local and co-operative evangelism, large numbers of people may turn to Christ and be added to the church. And what co-operative evangelism does is to add a further dimension of size to ongoing local church and personal evangelism. That was one effect of Mission England and Mission to London; in a short time many millions heard the gospel, and well over 100,000 responded to Billy Graham's preaching and to that of Luis Palau. It was a response of revival dimensions.

But *a revival does not stop when the evangelist finishes his work*. What is seen to a limited extent during evangelism happens extensively and continuously in revival.

If Mission England and Mission to London had been ongoing, their effects could perhaps have reached revival dimensions both in the church and in society. But like most evangelism in modern Britain, they were one-off efforts—we worked ourselves up in preparation and prayer to a climax, and then went back to our previous agendas. So the momentum of personal evangelism on a mass scale has generally not continued. Certainly the sense of God-awareness in society that was a feature of those events has declined. In most cases those who heard the gospel and did not respond to it have not continued to seek God and listen to his word.

Yet, though evangelism can take place without revival, you can't have revival without evangelism. In revival, evangelism is spontaneous. It's like internal combustion. People are converted in their thousands in a short space of time; and society's standards begin to be significantly affected as a result. During a spiritual awakening, you don't have to labour and exhort people in order to generate a desire to witness. The Spirit of God makes people want to share their faith and introduce others to the living God.

Revival is not meetings

A feature of revival is that there are many meetings. Some of them go on for hours, or even days! In the revival that swept Cornwall in the middle of the nineteenth century, William Haslam led one meeting that went on for eight days without a break. And that was just one meeting out of many.

But in some North American contexts the word 'revival' is used as if it meant exactly the same as 'evangelistic meeting'. You see advertisements for a 'revival crusade'—'Revival held here every Wednesday.' But both are loose usages of the word.

Some Pentecostal groups, too, advertise 'revival meetings'. Presumably this means that they have experienced revival in the past and have used the word 'revival' now in the hope that at the meetings, God's power to revive will be demonstrated once again.

But such a meeting could never be seen as part of a general spiritual awakening in the sense that I have used the word 'revival' so far: a spiritual awakening that affects the church and its surrounding community.

Revival is neither an organisation nor a mission

Sometimes evangelists use the word 'revival' as part of their organisation's name: 'The Joe Bloggs Revival Crusade.' But nobody can organise a revival. It can't be made to happen by efficient planning. We may fulfil the conditions for it by what we do in response to the ministry of the Holy Spirit, but the outpouring of that same Spirit—which is the hallmark of revival—is a sovereign work of God.

Biblical revival

We've seen what revival is not. So, what *is* revival? Let's see what the Bible has to say.

Old Testament revival

The word is used in Psalm 85: 'Will you not revive us again, that your people may rejoice in you?' (Ps 85:6). It is the heart-cry of God's people. In the past, they have experienced his forgiveness; now they are asking again for God to take away his displeasure over their sin. 'Restore us again, O God our Saviour' (v 4).

The psalm speaks of salvation, love, faithfulness, righteousness, goodness, peace and glory, and it ends with the words: 'Righteousness goes before him and prepares the way for his steps.' This is the vocabulary of the reviving work of the Spirit of God.

Hosea uses the same vocabulary. 'Come, let us return to the Lord . . . After two days he will revive us; on the third day he will restore us, that we may live in his presence' (Hos 6:1–2). There are those words again: 'return', 'revive' and 'restore'. For Hosea, 'revive' means 'make live again, or have new life'.

The Bible provides other evidence that such spiritual revival happened in Israel's history. When the people had fallen into apostasy; when the temple had been allowed to fall into disrepair; when idolatry and ignorance of God were plain to see; when the law was neglected or wilfully disobeyed—in such conditions God intervened afresh in the affairs of his people, and brought them back to the knowledge of himself and relationship with him that was their birthright. When he did so, he did not just intervene in the case of individuals. He intervened on a grand scale, swiftly righting wrongs and leaving nobody in the nation unaware of what was going on. And with the people's response came manifestations of the power of God (see 2 Chronicles 15,29–30; 2 Kings 23; Nehemiah 8–9).

New Testament revival

In two places in the New Testament we see something of the significance of revival. The first is in Acts 3:19–21:

> Repent, then, and turn to God, so that your sins may be wiped out, that times of refreshing may come from the Lord, and that he may send the Christ, who has been appointed for you—even Jesus. He must remain in heaven until the time comes for God to restore everything, as he promised long ago through his holy prophets.

Here we read of repentance, restoration, refreshing— reviving—and the 'sending' of Christ. 'Times of refreshing' from the Lord probably means more than we understand by 'conversion'. 'Times' is plural, whereas conversion, even though it is part of a process, is a single act.

The second significant New Testament reference is in Acts 2. Clearly, when the Holy Spirit was 'poured out' on the Day of Pentecost, it was a unique occasion and a very important one. It had a particular place in the promises of Christ, and it followed very shortly after his Resurrection and Ascension. It was part of that unique sequence of events.

Yet I don't believe that the outpouring of the Spirit was a once-for-all historical event. Jesus' promise of power

(Acts 1:8) was not only foundational to the church, but was also an essential element in its continuing power to witness. So we must see the Pentecost outpouring as something that will be necessary at other times in history, in order to achieve for future generations the expression of supernatural growth and release from fear that the early apostles experienced.

Hence the importance of waiting (1:4), of prayer (1:14), of unity (2:1) and of repenting. The first word of the gospel (2:38) has to be seen in the context not only of the initial outpouring of the Spirit, but also of subsequent ones. Edwin Orr comments:

> The major marks of an evangelical awakening are always some repetition of the phenomena of the Acts of the Apostles followed by the revitalising of nominal Christians and by bringing outsiders into vital touch with the divine dynamic, causing all such awakenings—the Spirit of God.[3]

The events recorded in the Acts have been repeated in full or lesser degree in the awakenings of past centuries. The same Spirit of God who moved the apostles has wrought his mighty works in the centuries before our own. The results have been the same. The effects have been wider than any the apostles could have dreamed of in their day.

The supernatural manifestations of the Holy Spirit's outpouring recorded in the early chapters of Acts have been repeated at various times through the centuries, and are being repeated in our own day in many parts of the world.

As I read about contemporary and historical awakenings, I find that all of them have a supernatural dimension, brought about by the sovereign work of God. Those influenced by the outpouring of the Spirit are affected in a way they have never experienced before, and appear to remain so for the rest of their lives.

In every case, man is surprised by what happens; by the scale of it, by its geographical extent, by its effect on the church, and by its consequences in society as a whole.

As Orr has said:'Revival produces an extraordinary burden of prayer, an unusual conviction of sin, an uncanny sense of the presence of God, resulting in repentance, confession, reconciliation and restitution with great concern for the salvation of sinners near at hand and far away.'[4]

Put simply revival is, according to D M Panton, 'the inrush of the Spirit of God into a body that threatens to become a corpse'. Dr J I Packer has said:

> In revival the saints are suddenly roused from a state of torpor and lethargy by a new and overwhelming awareness of the reality of spiritual things and of God. They are like sleepers now shaken awake and half blinded by the unaccustomed glare of the sun. They hardly know for a moment where they are. They now see everything as they never saw it before.[5]

What then should be our definition of the word 'revival'?

As we have seen, it's almost impossible to express the totality of what happens in a work of God. But we've seen a number of aspects which are certainly *part* of what happens.

So I would like to draw the various threads together and propose a working definition of 'revival'. I want to use the word in this book to mean 'the outpouring of the Holy Spirit, effecting the reviving of the church and the bringing to new life of large numbers of people in the surrounding community'.

It doesn't cover everything that the word expresses, but it indicates the emphases which I want to explore in the chapters that follow.

Notes

1. Arthur Wallis, *Rain From Heaven* (Hodder & Stoughton, 1979), p 15.
2. J Edwin Orr, *The Flaming Tongue* (Moody, 1973), p vii.
3. *ibid*.
4. J Edwin Orr, *The Outpouring of the Spirit in Revival and Awakening and Its Issue in Church Growth*, p4.
5. J I Packer (source unknown).

3
Doubts and Disagreements

Watch some people when they come into contact with revival, and you'll see their expectancy and excitement growing. Stories of God's extraordinary power and presence leave them open-mouthed. Goose-pimples appear. Their pulse quickens. 'Is God going to do it here? Now? In my lifetime?'

Watch others listening to the same stories, however, and you'll see disbelief and scepticism: 'Stories like that are always exaggerated. They're all full of evangelistic embellishment.' Often there is an implication that it's just emotionalism, or fantasy, or otherworldliness.

'The revival you're talking about happened in another country, another culture, another time,' say these sceptics. 'It's hardly relevant to us in the twentieth century. This is Western civilisation. We've got a long-established church. God doesn't *need* to do it here! In any case,' they argue, 'he's saying something quite different to the church today.'

Most people who talk like that live in situations very far from revival. Many of their congregations exist on a diet of failure, back-breaking work, countless setbacks, weakness in the fellowship, division and constant criticism. So revival is not just a remote possibility—it's a threatening one. 'If all we've heard about revival happens here, we'll have even more problems to deal with. We won't be able to cope!'

Ministers already wilting and overworked quail before the prospect of early-morning prayer gatherings, sacrificial living, long meetings, a massive influx of new and untaught Christians, and an expanding church roll. Faced with that prospect they opt for 'gradual growth', within manageable limits, rather than an explosion of new life.

Revival means renewal of life, and life means energy. It is true that revival delivers the church from the problems created by apathy and deadness, but it is equally true that revival plunges the church into a welter of new problems created by the torrential overflow of disordered and undisciplined spiritual vitality. In a revival, the saints are swept off their feet; they lose their sense of proportion. They fall into pride, delusions, unbalance, censorious modes of speech, extravagant forms of action. Unconverted persons are caught up in what is going on; they feel the power of truth, though their hearts remain unrenewed; they become 'enthusiasts', harsh and bitter, fierce and vain-glorious, cranky and fanatical. Satan keeps step with God, actively perverting and caricaturing all that the Creator is doing. A revival accordingly, is always a disfigured work of God, and the more powerful the revival, the more scandalizing disfigurements we may expect to see. Hence we cannot wonder if the revival comes to be bitterly opposed by respectable church members of limited spiritual insight, on account of the excesses linked with it; nor can we be surprised to find—as we regularly do—that many ministers stand aloof from the revival, and even preach against it and try to suppress it, on the grounds that it is not a spiritual phenomenon at all.[1]

Revival does cause problems. There has always been a tendency for division in the church, and some groups seem to remain untouched by the Spirit. And it seems that revival, paradoxically, divides as well as unites.

On one hand, Christians are united in times of revival by the Spirit, in prayer and in other ways. For example, in the second Great Awakening in 1858 both Arminians and Calvinists—traditionally deeply opposed to each other doctrinally—found common ground. The Arminians prayed in most Calvinistic fashion for God to begin and continue a sovereign work, and the Calvinists spent long hours seeking him and calling on him for an outpouring, and then worked like Arminians for the salvation of souls! And today charismatic, Pentecostal, evangelical, Reformed and many more Christians all want to see revival.

Yet, at the same time, revival is divisive. For example, some Restorationists today believe that God is renewing New Testament structures; if we get those right, then the church will grow. Others, who are very denominationally orientated, believe that they already have the right structures. But if revival comes, structures may in any case be blown apart by God's new work; so an inbuilt reserve and explicit coolness about revival persists.

Consequently there are two different attitudes to revival. Some people long for it; they've had a vision for it, they dream about it, they have a burden from God to pray for it. But others say that the first group is living in cloud-cuckoo land; they themselves don't want revival to come, because they fear it will lead to extremes, or will even die an early death. 'If it's going to come, it will come,' they say. 'We needn't spend our time talking, thinking and praying about it. God is more interested in what we're doing right now.'

Let's look more closely at four particular elements of the negative feelings which are expressed about spiritual awakening.

1. 'It's an unreal expectation'

I've only recently become aware of this argument—mainly because I have been a target of it. So I have had to examine it honestly.

It argues that people who are looking for revival tend to look back at the past. Welsh Christians, for example, have for years been accused of looking back nostalgically to the revival of 1904–5, instead of living in the real world of spiritual decline and churches closing down.

Or else it's said that 'revival people' tend to look at what God is doing somewhere else in the world— particularly if it's spectacular and sensational—rather like the person who always thinks the grass in next door's lawn is greener.

In both cases, critics accuse revival people of believing that revival can be had anywhere, just by repeating what has been done in the past; or that people who pray for revival, who write about it, speak about it, talk about or even prophesy about it, have got their heads in the clouds. They are accused of fantasising.

You can understand why such criticisms are made. Very few people living in Europe have experienced a spiritual awakening. Europe—apart from small areas reported in Norway, Rumania and the Hebrides—is the unrevived continent. So some feel that interest in revival is an unreal preoccupation because they have no experience of revival to relate it to. For them, it's something which hasn't been seen in Britain for eighty years.

And yet our isolation is a recent development. In the American revival of 1859, for example, news of what was happening there was shared at meetings in all four countries of the United Kingdom. 'This intelligence quickened the prayer-life of intercessors who flocked to prayer meetings in an unusual way.'[2]

The prayer meetings were not just directed towards the revival of the church. They were directed towards evangelism, too, and that in turn led to social action. The cumulative effect, as the revival caught fire, was a variety of extraordinary happenings. But underpinning that was a prayer movement, and it was the sharing of news that sparked it off.

And the question has to be asked: Why aren't we sharing like that today? When it does happen, it whets people's appetites; it leads, hopefully, to increased prayer and seeking God. So why aren't we spreading the news of God's workings today?

I think the answer is probably that it is yet another example of how the church has been affected by social change. We hear so much news today of startling and horrific things going on in other parts of the world. We get into the habit of insulating ourselves, of learning not to make a connection between what is going on *there*, and our own way of life *here*.

But what is going on elsewhere is not an illusion or a fantasy. It is happening in a world of which we are part. Only our own lack of faith and obedience hinder the movement of the Spirit here in the same way as he is moving in other places.

After all, is it unreal to look for something that we haven't yet experienced but which, we know from the Bible and from history, is one of God's ways of intervening in our world? Is it any more unreal than looking forward in anticipation to the second physical coming of Christ for his church? That hasn't happened at all; but we accept it as biblical doctrine!

2. 'It doesn't last'

Some Christians who want to see a permanent work of God criticise past revivals because they lacked permanence. Like Halley's Comet, they were seen for a brief period and then disappeared for decades.

Some are suspicious of evangelistic crusades for the same reason. They argue that such crusades create a temporary, and therefore false, expectation of church life. Excitement at every meeting, choirs, good music, appearances of personalities—these are not the stuff of regular, church-based ministry.

The implication of this argument is that what we are used to is 'normal' in some absolute sense, and that what we experience only occasionally is 'abnormal'. But that is not necessarily true. For example, in North America many churches accept as normal a style of evangelism which most British churches have only encountered through Billy Graham's ministry. For us it is extraordinary. But for them it is normal to have large choirs and orchestras, appearances made by well-known personalities, preaching of evangelistic fervour and 'appeals'.

It all depends on your perspective. Can it be that what we readily call 'normal' in our church life is actually 'subnormal'? If instead we looked on revival as the divinely-inspired norm for church life, we would be better able to sustain revival and all that it means for ongoing church growth.

Yet the witness of history is that revivals come to an end. Why is that the case? Why do revival phenomena cease?

We can't blame God for it; there are some obvious reasons.

Revival doesn't last when sin is tolerated and God's glory becomes tarnished

Sin is a product of the human condition. Its presence is the result of satanic activity and opposition; he will oppose any genuine work of God in any way he can. So if he can cause the instruments of God to become soiled by inducing them to give in to their fallenness, he will make their ministry ineffective.

There is enough evidence today, outside revival, of God's glory becoming tarnished. Some Christian leaders have become compromised by money, sex or power. Their ministry is spoiled and God's name is dishonoured. But that doesn't lead us to do away with Christian ministry, nor to deny its place in the church. And when Satan succeeds in disrupting the progress of a spiritual awakening, we ought not to assume that revival itself is invalidated.

Secondly,

Revival doesn't last if there is division in the church

It is generally believed that the decline of the Welsh revival of 1904–5 was due to theological disputes about tongues-speaking and other manifestations associated with the baptism of the Spirit. Division followed; the apostolic denomination began at that time.

Thirdly,

Lack of prayer contributes to the decline

'Revival is born in prayer, is sustained by prayer, and continues so long as revival prayer continues.'[3] So it follows that if God's people do not continue in prayer, perhaps because complacency creeps in, then the intensity of God's blessing will diminish.

A difficult question lies behind this issue. Which comes first: revival or prayer? If it's prayer, does that mean (as Finney suggests) that our fulfilling of the conditions creates the climate for revival? I don't believe that if we pray a great deal and organise prayer meetings, revival will be guaranteed. But I *do* believe that when we respond to the prompting of the Holy Spirit about prayer—prayer that is both a prelude to, and feature of, revival—then God is working sovereignly.

Revival isn't God's work alone, if by that is meant that we are robots or puppets with no minds of our own. What happens is that man and God are co-operating together on God's agenda and God's timetable. And so long as we are in step with God, revival can be continuous.

But alas! we tend to fall away, and as a result revival falls away. When prayer is not a continuing priority, we are actually allowing the Enemy a little more leeway to do his devilish work. But prayer helps to keep him at bay; tied up, restricted and held back.

We can find an example of this in the experiences of the Children of Israel and God's dealings with them. At various times he spoke to them. He was active in their midst. He guided them. They were his people enjoying the symbol, and at times the reality, of his presence. He did mighty deeds among them. Yet, despite their heritage, they still rebelled and went their own way. They allowed the Law and the temple worship to fall into disrepute.

The people of God today very often do the same. Despite all that God has given to his church, we are still— as individuals and sometimes as denominations—prone to rebel; to go our own way, follow our own prejudices, be diverted into extremes of heresy or, by sheer neglect, lose sight of some aspect of God's truth.

In revival, the Spirit often re-emphasises elements that the church has allowed to become very low priorities. Revival is his means of correcting us as a body; of correcting the imbalances and, in the process, blessing a great many people. If it doesn't last, it's our fault—not God's.

Sometimes there are sociological causes of the decline of revival

Often revival precedes a time of fierce persecution or social upheaval. Such a time can produce a preoccupation with sheer survival that can have a dampening effect on revival fires. On the other hand, persecution is sometimes a means of purifying the church, which actually grows more rapidly because of it.

Such social implications of revival (a more prominent presence and impact of the church in society) are based on transformations in the lives of individuals, and when individuals fail, the social transformations fail. In the book *Finney on Revival*, Shelhamer gives fifteen reasons for the cessation or decline of revival. They are all to do with human weakness, and include: pride about the revival, proselytising for one's own congregation or denomination, loss of brotherly love, inability to adapt to what God is doing, and lack of dependence on the Spirit.[4]

Yet revivals may seem to fail even when no obvious spiritual decline is present. I mentioned earlier that the Welsh revival is often criticised as short-lived. In *The Flaming Tongue*, Orr shows that the fervour and extraordinary happenings in Wales began to wane in 1905. At that time, a climate of criticism developed against Evan Roberts, the leader of the revival, from both secular and religious quarters, and on a variety of fronts. It was not that Roberts was unspiritual, nor that his own Christian life was in a mess. On the contrary, it seems that those of whom God makes particular use become targets for those who disapprove of what God is doing, and Roberts was no exception.

The criticisms took their toll. Little was heard of Roberts in public ministry after 1906. Did that mean that the revival had failed? In many ways, no. The Welsh revival may have been short-lived in Wales, but its effects were far-reaching throughout the United Kingdom and in other countries. It seemed that God took burning coals from Wales and used them to ignite fires in many parts of the world.

Revival and its effects live on in those who are brought to new life in Christ. The glow in their eyes and the awareness of being a part of a supernatural movement of God in history never leave them. Revival lives on in the experience of those churches which saw God work in power and received a large influx of new life. In Wales, churches remained filled to capacity for twenty years or more.

But revival rarely lasts into subsequent generations. It can't be passed on by hearsay or heredity to a new generation that knows nothing of the circumstances, central characters or immediate consequences of the revival. It is evangelism, not revival, which passes the message on to other generations.

And yet evangelism is fuelled by revival. The modern missionary movement owes much of its early zeal to the revivals of the nineteenth century and of 1904. And evangelism reaches countries which themselves then experience revival. Nagaland, a state to the North-East of India, began to experience revival in the 1960s. The Nagas are still in a state of revival and 85% of the population today are Christians.[5] The East African revival continued for many years, even into the reign of Idi Amin, and when Norman Grubb wrote during that period he called his book *Continuous Revival*.

3. 'It's open to counterfeit'

Yes—and so is everything else to do with Christianity! Satan is a deceiver, the master forger. He isn't capable of originality or creativity—so he copies. And he does it so skilfully that even the very elect are deceived (Mt 24:24).

Pseudo-Christianity comes in many forms. Cults, the occult, heresies, false religion, unbiblical practices—even plausible, biblically-based practices done without the Spirit!

Wherever you find the real thing, the counterfeit will

not be far away. Tares grow with the wheat; Judas Iscariot was one of the Twelve; Satan was a serpent in the Garden of Eden. But the reverse is also true. If something is being counterfeited—and every revival has had its share of aberrations—then there must be plenty of the real thing around as well!

4. 'It only encourages extremism and emotionalism'

The church has always suffered from extremists: either those whose character and personality produce excitable conduct and enthusiastic over-the-top sensationalism, or those whose dour outlook on life puts dampers on the work of God. We will always have the proverbial optimists or the kill-joy pessimists. And revival doesn't cause either of them.

However, because of the extraordinary nature of what often happens in revival, both extremes have a field day. Both seize the opportunity to express their exuberance or their negativism.

There is a place for both in the family of God. Without the optimist, little would happen by way of pioneering fresh visions or ideas. The church *needs* those who 'against hope believe'. But it also needs the person who will always ask the awkward question, whose attitude will put necessary brakes on over-enthusiastic and some-times ill-advised actions. What it does *not* need are the people whose extremism results in isolation, so that they are always apart from the rest of the church, doing their own thing.

Many forms of respectable Christian activity have been labelled 'emotionalism'. Billy Graham meetings, weddings, funerals, baptisms, celebrations, praise-and-prayer evenings, Bible weeks and many more have had the accusation levelled at them. Yet emotion is part of our human make-up, and to repress or ignore it is to risk unbalanced character development and church practice. Jesus wept at Lazarus' grave; he was *moved* with compassion (or, groaned inwardly) at the sight of the multitudes who were like sheep without a shepherd. If *he*, deity clothed in humanity, knew emotion and expressed it— then so should we.

But we can be emotional without risking sheer emotionalism. By 'emotionalism' I mean deliberately playing on people's emotions, whipping up religious fervour, or setting out to excite people. When that happens, the human element has taken control, and the spiritual element has been pushed into the back seat.

In times of revival, it's the other way round. But emotion isn't excluded. Is it not an exciting and emotional thing to see God at work in power and glory? To see people in their thousands turning to God? To be overcome by the awesome presence of the risen Christ?

Many congregations are not used to hearing about 'prostrations, faintings, prolonged periods of excitable praise and burdened praying'. But when God takes the stage, anything can happen!

Notes

1. J I Packer (source unknown).
2. J Edwin Orr, *The Second Evangelical Awakening* (Marshall Pickering, 1949), p 247.
3. Anon.
4. E E Shelhamer, *Finney on Revival* (Marshall Morgan and Scott).
5. Taken from a report of the Nagaland Baptist Church 1983.

4
God of Surprises

He longs to do much more than our faith has yet allowed
To thrill us and surprise us with his sovereign power.
Where darkness has been darkest the brightest light will shine
His invitation comes to us, it's yours and it is mine.[1]

God's ways are higher than our ways, and his thoughts
are higher than our thoughts. He works all things after
the counsel of his own will. He works in the realm of his
own knowledge, not ours.

All of which should lead us to expect that when God
takes the stage, things are going to happen that we are not
conditioned to expect. Even in human family life, a
loving parent or husband will often create a surprise just
for the joy of giving pleasure. In poor families it may be a
very modest surprise, in rich ones it may be extravagant;
but either way, it reflects something of the character of
the person who gave it.

God's abundant power

God has all power at his disposal. Out of his grace, love
and kindness, he can do anything he wants, whenever he

43

wants to. And it is his character to do immeasurably
more than we ask or think. Someone once wrote:

> We are profoundly impressed with the unlimited resources of
> the God of the Bible; He never does anything small; when He
> makes an ocean He makes it so deep that no man can fathom
> it.
>
> When He makes a mountain He makes it so large than no
> one can weigh it.
>
> When He makes flowers, He scatters multiplied millions of
> them where there is no one to admire them but Himself.
>
> When He makes grace, He makes it without sides or
> bottom, and leaves the top off.
>
> Instead of giving salvation with a medicine dropper, He
> pours it forth like a river.

He is a God of abundance, of overflowing, of overwhelming, of immense power, majesty and might; a
God of the much more, of the unfathomable, of the
immeasurable, of the impossible!

Power like that was demonstrated in the ministry of
Jesus. It was the power of a supernatural God working in
natural circumstances, and men were left in awe and
amazement. When he calmed the storm, his disciples
were astonished, and exclaimed, 'What kind of man is
this?' (Mt 8:27). When he healed the paralytic, the crowd
were 'filled with awe; and they praised God' (Mt 9:8).
When he cast out the demon from the dumb, demon-
possessed man, 'the crowd was amazed, and said
"Nothing like this has ever been seen in Israel."' (Mt
9:33).

He showed his authority over the elements, over
sickness and over demons. It was his authority that made
its mark on those who witnessed his mighty power. He
was sure of his God and the power vested in himself. And
when we too move into the full authority and power of
the Spirit, we may ourselves demonstrate the authority of
God; though we would have to confess, as Peter did, that

it was not by our own power or godliness that we had done it. 'It is Jesus' name and the faith that comes through him that has given this complete healing' (Acts 3:16).

In the Old Testament, God surprised Jacob when he wrestled with him all night. He surprised Moses when he appeared in the burning bush. He surprised Gideon when he brought about a mighty victory with Gideon's tiny army of 300 men against 135,000 Midianites. And God surprised Elijah, Ezekiel, Isaiah and Jeremiah—men who received a visitation from God that prepared them for what he was about to say or do in their day.

That is how it has been in times of revival. There is a release of divine power then that leaves people amazed. The heavens are opened, God comes down, he clothes himself again in our humanity, but it is his deity rather than our humanity that is seen. So often in Christian work, it is the other way round. But in revival God makes himself known, whether it be to many or to few. He pours out his Spirit, and everybody knows that God is among them.

The element of surprise is always present in revival. Revival can't be programmed or planned. Even though Charles Finney maintained that revival is 'nothing more than the right use of the appropriate means', it must be acknowledged that all true outpourings of the Spirit in revival are a sovereign intervention of God. It is he who is pouring out his Spirit; he who is generating a state of revival; he who is producing a spiritual awakening. Men and women of all ages co-operate, yes, but it is God who takes the initiative.

When God does take the stage, his method of working is always surprising and a cause for wonder, but it is different every time. Though there are often elements in common—such as prayer, personal holiness and a sense of the presence of God—the particular emphasis, or geographical extent, or length of time, all vary.

In one revival he may use a particular personality; in another, no single person stands out. In one case, the social repercussions can be extensive; in another, the result is specific to one aspect of community life. Not all revivals are marked by charismatic manifestations such as tongues or healings. Not all revivals have had a profound effect on social conditions—though the effects in terms of spontaneous evangelism are always present. Sometimes a revival takes place while persecution is happening; sometimes it is followed by persecution.

Just as God has various methods in revival, so do his methods of bringing people into a relationship with himself through his Son vary.

He may choose to work without any human agent, or he may work through a massive Billy Graham crusade. He may use television, or a book; a gospel rock concert or a choral concert; the words of a friend or the silent witness of a praying relative. He may make use of the normal activities of the church, or he may simply put somebody in the right place at the right time. A dream, a vision, the inner voice of the Spirit; a word of knowledge (as happened with the woman at the well, in John 4); by a great variety of methods, God still speaks and works 'at sundry times and in divers manners' (Heb 1:1, AV).

A transformed society

We have already seen that the Welsh revival's effects lasted in the church for many years, and its repercussions were worldwide. But what amazing things happened in the space of less than a year in Wales! By the end of 1905, one third of the 2.22 million population were registered communicants of the Anglican and Free Churches. In six months, 100,000 were born again, and in addition to these, church members who had previously been only nominal Christians came into contact with living

Christianity. In some rural mining communities, 75% of the population were counted as church members, though Cardiff could only boast of 17%. In Anglican services, there were outbursts of spontaneous prayer and praise.

Out of the Revival came a social awakening in Wales, in Cardiff taking the form of a purity crusade directed by the Cardiff Citizens' Union aimed at suppressing drunkenness, immorality and gambling, successful in amending criminal law and forcing the closing of brothels, shutting up sixty taverns and preventing forty more from opening.[2]

The Registrar-General's statistics on illegitimate births showed a percentage decline in every county in Wales, as much as 40% in Radnor and Merioneth in the year following, and from 9.2 to 8.4 per thousand in Glamorgan, 1904–7. The great wave of sobriety which swept over the country caused severe financial losses to men in the liquor trade, and closed many of the taverns.

Swansea County Police Court announced to the public that there had not been a single charge for drunkenness over the 1905 New Year holiday weekend, an all time record in fact; in the Welsh metropolis, the Cardiff police reported a 60% decrease in drunkenness and 40% fewer people in jail at the New Year also.[3]

Stocks of Welsh and English Bibles were sold out. Prayer meetings were held in coal mines, in trains and trams and places of business. The works managers bore testimony of the change of conduct of their employees. The magistrates in several places were presented with white gloves, signifying that there were utterly no cases to try.

The life of the coal pits was transformed. Not only did workers and management engage in prayer meetings on the company's time which was being put to such good use in the ordinary hours of activity, but the pits themselves showed silent indicators of the new spirit—with texts chalked upon ventilating doors for all to see who passed that way.[4]

The Revival has caused the mightiest upheaval in the social life of the people apart from the religious aspect, that living generations have ever seen ... The movement is elevating thousands of individual men and women, and the nation, to that degree, must be the gainer. Every week of my life I am brought into touch with hundreds, if not thousands of people in one way or another, and the change I have witnessed as a consequence of the influence of this Revival is nothing short of a miracle.[5]

The vision of Evan Roberts that a hundred thousand people would be won to the churches in Wales was fully realised in a matter of months. At the time, the Revival united the denominations as one body, filled the chapels nightly, renewed family ties, changed life in mines and factories, often crowded streets with huge processions, abated the social vices and diminished crime.[6]

But surprising occurrences did not only happen in the Welsh revival. God has worked marvellously in almost every continent and in every culture. And whenever the power of God is revealed, people are always left awe-struck.

Orr chronicled one such event in South Africa in the mid-twentieth century. Nicholas Bhengu, a Pentecostal African evangelist, was active among the Zulus soon after the Second World War.

One day a crowd of over 7,000 were assembled in the open air. While they were singing a simple Christian chorus, the Holy Spirit fell upon them, just as He did upon the household of Cornelius when Peter was preaching in Acts 10. That was at half-past ten in the morning, and that great crowd were still there when darkness fell. Small boys of just twelve years talked in tongues and prophesied. It was impossible for Bhengu or anybody else to preach. As on the day of Pentecost, 'it was noised abroad' and people gathered from all over to see what the noise was. When they came into the revival atmosphere these sightseers too were converted. The numbers continued to increase and the Lord continued to save and baptise them with the Holy Ghost and fire.

The people were so under the power of God that they could not walk, many of them were prostrated and lay as though they were dead. Bhengu sent for buses to come and take the people to their homes, but as soon as the bus drivers and conductors tried to pick them up they themselves came under the power of the Holy Spirit. They said to Bhengu, 'As soon as we touch them this comes into us.' Very many of these bus drivers and conductors were converted. The result of the revival was such that a local theatre, which had been very popular, had to close down because no one wanted to go any more. The owners begged Nicholas Bhengu and his followers to rent it from them.[7]

Kurt Koch was a chronicler of spiritual phenomena. He is reputed to have said that in the Zulu revival completely ignorant heathens, on opening themselves to Christ, were instantly given the ability to read, and in some cases to write.

The Spirit's work

From my own reading of many accounts of revival, I believe that there is a correlation between the supernatural ministry of the Holy Spirit and the extraordinary and unpredictable responses of the people who are affected.

First comes the *revival of Christians*—a return to prayer, a renewed sincerity in holy living, an appetite for God's word and a hunger for his work. This may find expression in times of prolonged calling upon God in prayer and fasting.

Then comes a *visitation from on high*. God intervenes! That is where the element of surprise begins. It may start in a single meeting; it may happen simultaneously in several places. It may be spread through the sole influence of the Holy Spirit, or by those who have been affected themselves preaching to others. It may strike the non-Christian community with awesome power, so that hundreds and thousands seek God as if driven by an invisible force.

Sin is disowned. Confession and repentance are followed by restitution. People hunger for God. They don't want to leave the atmosphere of what God is doing, so meetings last well into the night, for a whole day or for days on end. Often sleep is limited to a few hours. Consider this account from Wales in 1904:

> He came home from the early shift, washed off the coal-dust, put on his best clothes and took his wife and children to the nearby chapel, which was packed at four in the afternoon. Evan Roberts arrived about seven, made his way to the front of the big church, climbed over the knees of the people sitting around the pulpit, stood up and uttered but one word in Welsh, 'Let us pray.' Immediately prayer burst forth audibly and simultaneously from the vast crowd; but Evan Roberts took no further part in the extraordinary proceedings, making his way out about ten p.m. to pray all night in the quiet of his room. The meeting was continuing in full power at two a.m., when the family made its way out. The children were put to bed, but the miner dozed in the big chair by the fire till daybreak, went to work, returned home, took a bath, put on his best clothes, and took his family back to the chapel at four to the same meeting still going strong.[8]

Meetings for praise and prayer are often spontaneous, with no planning. Prayer is frequently simultaneous, just as it was in Acts 4 where 'they raised their voices together unto God'. People may lie prone on the floor, or lose consciousness, sometimes for several hours. There may be spiritual phenomena, like tongues, words of prophecy or proclamation and healings.

Then follows a phase of *evangelism and witness*, at both personal and large-scale levels. Certainly the new converts have a desire to share what God has done—but so do mature Christians, whose 'holy boldness' has taken on a new meaning.

So the message is shared near and far, and many more are brought to know Christ in a personal and life-changing way. Evangelism happens spontaneously as people 'gossip' the gospel.

In the Welsh revival the police had hardly anything to do but control the crowds attending church, and to send singing groups to sing at the services.

That is how God reveals his power at times of revival—'an arm that is not shortened that it cannot save'. God, who works in ways we can neither predict nor control, visits us when he wants to, how he wants to, and for as long as he wants to.

Like a tidal wave, his blessing breaks upon the shore. Other waves precede and follow. Many are influenced far away. It is like a dam overflowing; like a prolonged downpour, not just a shower; like a blaze of light that dispels the darkness.

His visitation is surprising—and it is also spontaneous; that seems to be another common denominator. There is spontaneity in worship, prayer, preaching and other church activities. Where there is an openness to revival, the most habit-bound congregation will be marked by a new spontaneity.

Revival is more than we could ever have dreamed of.

As the psalmist said: 'The Lord has done this, and it is marvellous in our eyes' (Ps 118:23).

Notes

1. Graham Kendrick, 'One Shall Tell Another' (Thankyou Music, 1981)
2. J Edwin Orr, *The Flaming Tongue* (Moody, 1973), p 18.

3. *ibid*.
4. ibid, p 19.
5. I R Govan, *Spirit of Revival* (Faith Mission, 1938), p 133.
6. J Edwin Orr, *op cit*, p 28.
7. Colin Whittaker, *Great Revivals* (Marshall Pickering, 1984), p 122.
8. J Edwin Orr, *op cit*, p 13.

Section II
Features of Revival

5
The Presence of God

Oh, that you would rend the heavens and come down, that the mountains would tremble before you! As when fire sets twigs ablaze and causes water to boil, come down to make your name known to your enemies and cause the nations to quake before you! For when you did awesome things that we did not expect, you came down, and the mountains trembled before you. Since ancient times no-one has heard, no ear has perceived, no eye has seen any God besides you, who acts on behalf of those who wait for him (Is 64:1–4).

In revival, God comes down. In a sense, he rends the heavens. He enters our world in power and authority. He visits communities, individuals, churches. The movement of his power and his Spirit is such that it is like a fire being set ablaze, like water boiling.

Once a blaze catches hold, once water starts to boil, there is heat, there is activity, there is power, there is cleansing and there is purification. Fire refines and purifies, it burns up the dross and the rubbish, and it warms and gives light.

One of the ways God chose to make his presence known was the burning bush encountered by Moses. It was burning, but it was not being burned up. The place was holy ground; Moses had to remove his shoes. The Bible tells us that 'Moses hid his face, because he was afraid to look at God' (Ex 3:6).

God came down when he met with Moses on the top of Mount Sinai, where the Lord called to him from the mountain and told him what he was to say to the people; then he gave him the Law. Moses ascended to the top of the mountain and God descended to it.

Moses made the ascent again and again, going back each time to the people to report what was happening. But finally he stayed on the summit for forty days and forty nights. God met with him there. He instructed him about the tabernacle and the offerings.

Then Moses came down from the mountain, and he found only idolatry and immorality. The tablets of the Ten Commandments were shattered. There was a plague throughout the camp. God had come down again—but this time he had come down in judgement over sin.

Yet he was open to the prayers of his servants Moses and Joshua. He came down once more, as Moses entered the makeshift tent outside the camp. The awesome presence of God was so real that when the Lord said, 'My Presence will go with you, and I will give you rest' (Ex 33:14), he wasn't just talking about the theological acceptance of the spiritual reality. He was going to be manifesting his presence in such a way that people could not look at Moses. 'When Aaron and all the Israelites saw Moses, his face was radiant, and they were afraid to come near him' (34:30).

And you will find that often, when God has wanted to demonstrate his presence in such a way that change—either in society or in an individual's sense of direction and purpose—would follow rapidly, he has revealed himself.

King David was somebody who knew a great deal about the presence of the Lord. He knew that presence in the guidance God gave him day by day. He knew it in the sense of power and victory God gave him in the battles he had to fight. He knew it in the intimacy of the relationship he experienced with God, and which he broke by his own sin. He records that knowledge in Psalm 51.

And he knew God's presence in the way God dealt with him personally. Because he knew of the omniscience of God, so far as it concerned him, he was able to say: 'Where can I go from your Spirit? Where can I flee from your presence?' (Ps 139:7). As far as that one man was concerned, God had come down.

In the presence of the Lord, sin is challenged. That's why David, when he was confronted by Nathan the prophet, was able to understand at last that his own transgression had caused God's presence to be withdrawn. Jonah, when he disobeyed God and refused to go to Nineveh, 'fled from the presence of the Lord' (Jon 1:3,10, AV).

In the New Testament, we read of demons trembling with fear at godhood present in Jesus, the Son of God, and pleading to be cast out of the man they were controlling and into a herd of pigs (Mk 5). It was the presence of God that they could not stand.

And Acts 3:19, which we have already considered, points to the meaning of revival: in the Authorized Version it speaks of 'times of refreshing from the presence of the Lord'. What the apostles experienced when the Spirit was poured out on the Day of Pentecost is typical of what happens in revival times. God came down. His Spirit was poured out. Demonstrations of God's supernatural power were taking place so often that the people around were 'utterly amazed'.

They didn't understand what was going on, so Peter explained to them that God had come down. He quoted from God's promise in the book of Joel:

I will pour out my Spirit on all people. Your sons and daughters will prophesy, your young men will see visions, your old men will dream dreams. Even on my servants, both men and women, I will pour out my Spirit in those days, and they will prophesy (Acts 2:17–18).

By quoting that, Peter was making the point that the Pentecost event was not a unique happening. God had already revealed that it would happen. In fact, he had occasionally given glimpses of what it was going to be like when it did happen.

And today God is still in the business of revealing his presence, of coming down, of appearing in glory and power, of astounding and amazing those who see it.

There are not too many instances of the presence of God being poured out so that whole geographical areas and sections of the population are influenced. Certainly in Scripture we find that God seems to make his presence known particularly to individuals. People like Isaiah, Jeremiah, Ezekiel and Daniel had extraordinary encounters with God.

Today he still reveals himself in that way, as many individuals can testify. They can point to God appearing to them, speaking to them, revealing himself in dreams and visions, and giving them a unique sense of direction.

The manifestation to individuals does seem to be a particular emphasis in God's revelation of himself. But that revelation is also given in ways that influence whole communities and entire geographic areas; and thereby men and women know that God is among them. When God comes like that, he doesn't tell people he is coming. There is no advance publicity machine. And, as we have seen, the suddenness of his coming sometimes takes people by surprise.

Yet it seems that the people he uses in such times are

people whose hearts have already been warmed by the Spirit of God, who have made the effort to seek the Lord, to fast and pray, to spend time in his presence. The people he uses are people who are open and honest about their own weakness and failure. They don't wilt under the guilt of it, but on the other hand they don't come to a holy God with presumption or flippancy.

Through those few, he is able to express himself and his power to many, many more.

Channels of blessing

In the Hebridean revival, two elderly sisters spent three nights every week praying by the peat fire in their cottage. Prostrate on the ground, they pleaded a single promise: 'I will pour water upon him that is thirsty and floods upon the dry ground.' In their eyes, it was the promise of a covenant-keeping God who could never break his word.

At the same time a group of young men were also seeking God. They knew of the desperate spiritual need of the people round them. All their efforts at changing matters had failed. Now they were seeking the Lord, and were determined to wait until he answered.

As they prayed, the words of Psalm 24 took on fresh meaning: 'Who shall ascend unto the hill of the Lord or who shall stand in his holy place? He that has clean hands and a clean heart.' And then one said, 'It seems so much sentimental humbug to be praying as we are praying, to be waiting as we are waiting, if we ourselves are not rightly related to God.' And then he prayed, 'Are my hands clean, is my heart pure?'

At that moment there came to them a realization of God, an awareness of his presence that lifted them from the sphere of the ordinary into the sphere of the extraordinary. Three of them fell prostrate on the floor: they realised at that moment that they were now moving not in the field of the natural but on the plane of the supernatural. Revival had come and the power that was let loose in that barn shook the whole community of Lewis.'[1]

In Duncan Campbell's words:

Revival is a community saturated with God. That is the difference between revival and successful evangelism. In successful evangelism you have 10, maybe 20 saved here or a 100 brought to Christ there but the community remains unchanged. Men move on to their Christless hells. But when God steps down, when hearts are made clean by Him, then He finds an avenue through which He can move; the community becomes saturated with God so that many of those who find the Saviour come into a saving relationship with him before they come near any church or place of meeting.[2]

At the first meeting that Duncan Campbell came to in the Hebridean revival,

a deacon declared, 'Mr Campbell, God is hovering over, He is going to break through.' But though it was a good meeting, with good singing and liberty in prayer and preaching, there was nothing more. At the end of the service however, the same deacon told Duncan, 'Do not be discouraged, He is coming, I hear already the rumbling of heaven's chariot wheels.' Then he suggested to the already exceedingly travel weary Duncan that they go and spend the night in prayer. About 30 of them retired to a nearby cottage. Duncan Campbell described what happened. 'God was beginning to move, the heavens were opening, we were there on our faces before God. Three o'clock in the morning came and GOD SWEPT IN. About a dozen men and women lay prostrate on the floor, speechless. Something had happened; we knew that the forces of darkness were going to be driven back, and men were going to be delivered. We left the cottage at 3 am to discover men and women seeking God. I walked along a country road, and found three men on their faces, crying to God for mercy. There was a light in every home, no one seemed to think of sleep.'

While Duncan and his friends gathered at the church later in the morning, the place was crowded. A stream of buses came from every part of the island, yet no one could discover who had told them to come. A butcher and his van brought 7 men from a distance of 17 miles. All 7 were gloriously converted. Now the revival was under way.

The Spirit of God was at work. All over the church men and women were crying for mercy, some fell into a trance, some swooned, many wept. Campbell pronounced the benediction and almost all left the chapel. Suddenly a young man began to pray, he was so burdened for the souls of his friends that he prayed for three-quarters of an hour, out loud. During this time the people returned to the church, joined by many others until there were twice as many outside as inside. In some amazing way the people gathered, from Stornoway, Ness and different parishes.

It was 4 am the following morning before Duncan pronounced the benediction for a second time.

Even then he was still unable to go to bed. As he was leaving the church a messenger told him, 'Mr Campbell, people are gathered at the police station from the other end of the parish. They're in great spiritual distress, can anyone come here and pray with them.' Campbell went, and what a sight met him. Under the starlit sky, he found men and women on the road, others by the side of the cottage, some behind a peat stack all crying to God for mercy. The revival had come.[3]

The presence of God had swept through.

That was 1949 in the Outer Hebrides. Let's go back a little further, back into the first Great Awakening that took place in the middle of the eighteenth century at the time of George Whitefield and Charles Wesley.

In June 1742 Whitefield arrived at the kirk-yard in Cambuslang in Scotland to witness a movement which far outdid anything he ever saw in America. To vast concourses of people he preached at 2, 6, and 9 pm. At 11 pm there was much weeping for an hour and a half. The local minister continued preaching after midnight, scarcely able to get the people to retire at 1 am.

On Saturday 9th July he preached to 20,000 on the 'preaching braes'. On Sunday 30,000 attended, 1,700 taking the sacraments, in two great tents. On 15th August, 12 assisting ministers held a second communion with upwards of 30,000 people attending. The effects of this work were felt all over Scotland. A dozen ministers held another communion service that began at 8.30 in the morning and concluded twelve hours later, a score of separate services having been held.[4]

The presence of God had come. His visitation had affected the community at large.

At the beginning of this century, a report appeared from a man called Seth Joshua who was a mentor of Evan Roberts, one of the key figures that God picked up and used in the revival that took place in Wales. His meetings at New Quay lasted far into the night. 'I cannot leave the building until 12 and even 1 o'clock in the morning,' wrote Joshua:

> I closed the service several times and yet it would break out again quite beyond the control of human power. A remarkable revival spirit was experienced in the place. I've never seen the power of the Holy Spirit so powerfully manifested among the people, as at this place just now.[5]

Later on it was the turn of Evan Roberts, who picked up the torch so to speak, with a real hunger and thirst for the outpouring of God's Spirit in revival. He was gripped with the Spirit of intercession. 'For ten or eleven years I have prayed for revival. Revival has been the passion of my heart,' he said. 'I could sit up all night to read and talk about revivals. ... It was the Spirit of God that moved me to think about revival.'[6]

At times, he was overwhelmed by the presence of God.

On October 31st, 1904, he felt that God was strongly urging him to return home to Loughor in South Wales.

He went straight home to his Pastor and asked permission to hold services for young people. After the adult prayer meeting, just 16 adults and one girl remained at Evans's invitation. He quietly explained why he had come home. He mentioned the promised revival. On Tuesday the 1st November, one day later, there were more present as he spoke on the importance of being filled with the Holy Spirit. He lay great emphasis on the work of the Holy Spirit. In later years he wrote,

'The baptism of the Holy Spirit is the essence of revival. Revival comes from a knowledge of the Holy Spirit and the way of co-working with Him which enables Him to work in Revival power. The primary condition of revival is therefore that Believers should individually know the baptism of the Holy Ghost.'

The following night for the first time he spoke on the four great points which became the important part of his message wherever he went throughout the whole period of the Welsh revival.

Firstly, if there is sin in your past that you've not confessed to God, you must put it away and be cleansed.

Secondly, if there is anything in your life that is doubtful, you must get rid of it. Have you forgiven everybody, everybody? If not, don't expect forgiveness for your own sins. Forgiveness must flow.

Thirdly, do what the Spirit prompts you. Obedience, prompt, implicit unquestioning obedience to the Spirit is important.

Fourthly, be prepared to confess Christ as your Saviour. There's a vast difference between *pro*fession of Christ and *con*fession. We can profess to be Christians, but it's not until we start to confess Him to others that it begins to have effect in the community.

Throughout the week, the meetings continued. He was invited to preach in the Sunday evening service the following week, and at the close of his message some 60 young people responded for salvation. Then he taught the people to pray. 'Send the Spirit now, for Christ's sake.'

It was after midnight before they dispersed; the Monday Prayer Meeting next evening was packed out. Evan Roberts read the last chapter of Malachi. The people were astonished at his boldness as he emphasized that this Scripture was going to be fulfilled right there in Loughor. This was the first time that the revival love song was sung, 'Here is love, vast as the ocean.' That meeting did not close until 3 am.

The next meeting, Tuesday 8th November, was just 9 days after he came back to Loughor. The atmosphere in the service was quite cold. Roberts agonized in prayer for God to melt the atmosphere with Christ's love. They were there until the early hours, but now the community was affected and at 6 am on the Wednesday morning people were awakened by the sound of crowds flocking to the early morning prayer meeting. The whole town was rapidly becoming a prayer meeting.[7]

It was not long before similar things were happening throughout Wales. It did not depend on Evan Roberts' presence or absence. What mattered was that God was there. And where there was a real sense of God's presence, people stayed at church meetings all night. They did not want to be away from what God was doing.

God's presence extended from the church buildings into the Welsh mines, as people prayed together underground. Entire rugby and soccer teams became Christians.

The presence of God was felt everywhere. The atmosphere was divinely charged. A miner who was converted in the revival once described it in the following graphic way. He said that he had been in the revival and he had also on one occasion been in an underground explosion in one of the local pits and there was not much to choose between the two! The atmosphere underground was charged with dust and methane gas, and the atmosphere in Wales in the revival was impregnated with the presence of God.[8]

Jonathan Edwards, writing about the revival that came to Northampton, Massachusetts in 1735, said: 'The town seemed full of the presence of God. It never was so full of love, nor of joy, and yet so full of distress as it was then. There were remarkable tokens of God's presence in almost every house.'[9]

God's presence is a presence that can be felt, not just in the cloistered surroundings of church meetings or in Bible conventions, but also in the community. 'Revival is a community saturated with the presence of God.'

Will *you* pray? Will you seek God, asking him to pour his presence out upon the church and upon the community?

'Come, Lord; quicken us, revive us—and visit us!'

Notes

1. Duncan Campbell, *The Price and Power of Revival* (Faith Mission), pp 50–52.
2. *ibid*.
3. Colin Whittaker, *Great Revivals* (Marshall Pickering, 1984), pp 159–160.
4. J Edwin Orr, *Re-study of Revival and Revivalism* (1981), p 4.
5. J. Edwin Orr, *The Flaming Tongue* (Moody, 1973), p 3.
6. *ibid*, p 4.
7. Colin Whittaker, *op cit*, pp 91–92.
8. *ibid*, p 94.
9. Jonathan Edwards, *Historical Collections of Accounts of Revival* (Banner of Truth, 1981), p 290.

6

The Holiness of God

In the last chapter, we saw that the presence of God is one of the hallmarks of revival. If that is so, then it follows that the holiness of God is another. God cannot be separated from his own holiness. When he speaks, when he visits a particular area, group of people, or individual, then he reveals the power of an omnipotent, supernatural God. People are left gasping in wonder, humbled in submission, redeemed and revolutionised in the way they live.

Why does this happen? It happens because the experience of revival is the experience of the Spirit of God, whose name is the *Holy* Spirit. Because the Spirit *is* holy, when he comes he brings something of the holy character of God with him. And during times of revival, when the Spirit is working, the holiness of God is very self-evident.

God's character is holy and righteous. It is as unlike our own as it could possibly be. Yet, another characteristic of God is that he wants our characters to become like his. So whether God is active in the life of a single individual, or moving in mighty power through a community, the Holy Spirit is radically changing people's hearts more and

more into the likeness of God's righteousness, and trans-
lating that righteousness into altered behaviour patterns
and transformed lives.

The Bible uses a financial metaphor: God's character of
righteousness is *credited to us* (see Romans 4:22–4). In the
process, he is remaking us in his own image. When God
created man in the beginning, he had complete fellowship
with him. There was no sin to bar the way. It was only
when Satan entered human history that fellowship with
God was broken and the image of God in mankind
spoiled. But in conversion, God is restoring human
beings to their rightful place; he is remaking them in his
image, renewing fellowship with them. In revival, the
same thing is happening, but on a much grander scale.
And because of that, we become much more aware of the
holiness of God, as we see it expressed in individual and
community life.

That is how God gives us the gift of his holiness.

Being holy

But there is a sense, too, in which holiness is something
we have to obtain by working for it. Paul suggests that
we should offer ourselves 'in slavery to righteousness
leading to holiness' (Rom 6:19). That involves commit-
ting our wills—we have to *resolve* to be holy.

Peter says that we should be holy for two reasons.
First, because God himself is holy (1 Pet 1:15–16); secondly,
because the Day of God is coming. We ought to live
'holy and godly lives' (2 Pet 3:11–12).

We are made holy, on one hand, by the fact that God
disciplines us so that we can 'share in his holiness', and on
the other hand we strive to make the presence of that
holiness in us a reality: we 'make every effort . . . to be
holy' (Heb 12:14).

One aspect of holiness is that it is the absence of sexual

uncleanliness, as Paul explains in 1 Thessalonians 4:3–7. God wants us to be holy, calls us to be holy, and equips us with his Spirit to make us holy. We 'perfect' that holiness, or bring it to maturity as a quality of life to be pursued, by keeping ourselves free from unholy practices, thoughts and situations (though not from people!).

But how often Christians have regarded 'holiness' as no more than a string of negative ideas! Some of us have grown up with lists of 'no-go areas'—no-go habits, no-go places and even no-go people. No wonder we have a negative view of holiness! The word badly needs to be redeemed and restored to its real, biblical meaning. It needs to be seen as something glorious; the expression of God's own character, with which he endows us as he gives us his Spirit.

God is making us like himself. He is giving us the capacity to be like him in character, in power, in creativity, in lifestyle—in all things. And that's a really positive thing.

Duncan Campbell remarks:

A God-sent revival must ever be related to holiness and real New Testament separation. Yes, that was the truth that they had discovered; revival was coming, God was going to be honoured, they were going to see men so supernaturally altered that holiness would characterise every part of their being, body, soul and spirit . . .

If the secret of holiness is in the complete filling of the soul with the life of Christ; if the baptism with the Holy Spirit is, in its final analysis the revelation of Jesus; if the beauty of Christian character comes from the incorporation of His personality in mine, surely the great need of the Christian church today is a clean heart.[1]

So 'holiness' means human beings bearing the personality of God. But how can we know what God is really like?

We can know that by looking at Jesus. He is 'holy, blameless, pure, set apart from sinners, exalted above the heavens' (Heb 7:26). He was spoken of as 'the Holy One'; he was sinless in character, thought and action; he was 'in the world, but not of it'. Yet he did not live in isolation from others. He exposed sin, just by being himself. 'If I had not come and spoken to them, they would not be guilty of sin. Now, however, they have no excuse for their sin ... If I had not done among them what no-one else did, they would not be guilty of sin' (Jn 15:22, 24).

Wherever holiness is found it has the same effect. It exposes unholy acts and unholy attitudes. And when God's holy character is reproduced in us, the Holy Spirit cleans up our minds and habits, and changes our behaviour and disposition. When this transforming power begins to affect the outside world as well, we see an upturn in the whole moral climate.

The Holy Spirit

Who then is the Holy Spirit who engineers this change?

The word 'holy' in the New Testament is always a translation of the same Greek word: *hagion*. It means 'physically pure, morally blameless or religious, and ceremonially consecrated'. Its exact meaning in a particular passage depends on the words that accompany it. Thus you will find holy people, holy places, holy temples, holy kisses, holy days.

The word 'Spirit' (or 'Ghost') translates the Greek word *pneuma*, which means 'wind or spirit'. The word is used throughout the New Testament to denote the human spirit, the Spirit of God, demonic or unclean spirits, Christ's Spirit, or Holy Spirit. So this is another word that takes its precise meaning from its context.

'God is spirit, and his worshippers must worship in

spirit and in truth' (Jn 4:24). We can only do that
when our human spirits are made holy. Worship isn't
merely a task of the mind, or even of the body; it is a
spiritual exercise. Those who perform that exercise are
spirits made alive, in truth, by the imparting of God's
Spirit.

So, when God moves in a person or in a community,
he breathes his wind, his Spirit, to bring life, just as he
did when he created man. But the Bible does not talk
about *a* spirit. It talks about *the*, *Holy*, Spirit. In other
words, the Holy Spirit expresses all the character of
God.

The coming of the Spirit therefore has implications for
us, for society and for the church. It was the same when
he came on the Day of Pentecost. The disciples were
affected first, then the people watching in open-mouthed
amazement, and then the church that came into existence
as a result of that outpouring.

What does God want to do in revival?

When God sends the Spirit in revival, what is it that he
intends to do? He wants to do three things.

God wants to change us as individuals

He wants to change our thinking about repentance and
confession. He has no use for blocked-up channels. If we
genuinely long to see the Spirit of God poured out in
revival, we ourselves must be prepared to change, and to
allow the Spirit to take away any attitudes, habits or
relationships that hinder him from working.

At this point, revival becomes costly. It's no good
pointing the finger at the things that are wrong with
other people if we're not prepared to allow God to shine
his searchlight on our own lives. Revival has to start
with ourselves. Then, as each of us responds to him,

we will become channels through whom God's word of
truth is communicated to others. That has been his
method in every revival: as the word has taken root in
individuals or small groups, others have been affected
by it.

So we must ask ourselves some hard questions. Most
of us hear God's word regularly, often in circumstances
where it is made particularly relevant to us; but when did
it last produce a response of obedience? If we were all
diligent listeners *and doers* of the word, we'd be in revival
tomorrow.

God is looking for people who are genuine, who are
honest, who are responsive to him, who will turn from
all sin and from the very appearance of sin. When he puts
his finger on a sore spot, it is vitally important that we
should open ourselves up to him and allow him to carry
out his cleansing, healing, restoring and forgiving work.
Whether it's a painful memory, a festering grievance, a
soured relationship, a critical spirit, an impure thought-
life, resentment, rejection, bitterness, pride ... it's essential that we should be vulnerable to God, that we should
confess what is wrong and then turn away from it.

Commenting on the Welsh revival, Dr Campbell
Morgan had this to say:

> The movement is characterized by the most remarkable
> confessions of sin, confessions that must be costly. I heard
> some of them who have been members of the church and
> officers of the church confessing hidden sins in their hearts,
> impurity committed and condoned, and seeking prayer for its
> putting away.[2]

In the East African revival that took place in Burundi,
God's work could be summed up by the phrase 'confession
is a bridge to fellowship'. The revival was famous for the
fact that Christians were confessing their sins to each
other. Fellowship was restored at a deep, personal level.

If God tells you that you must go to somebody and admit that you are in the wrong, are you prepared to do it? If it's going to make you look small in someone else's eyes, will you go through with it?

It is only when we climb down from our self-made pedestals and admit that we have faults, that we begin to build a bridge towards other people.

The sequence is described by James: 'The prayer offered in faith will make the sick person well; the Lord will raise him up. If he has sinned, he will be forgiven. Therefore confess your sins to each other and pray for each other so that you may be healed' (Jas 5:15–16).

When we don't confess, we don't pray. When we criticise and complain, we play into the hands of the enemy. Confession of sins comes before we pray for each other, and it's the prayer of 'a righteous man' that is powerful and effective.

In the East African revival

the principal emphasis was on repentance. Under the purging flame of the Holy Spirit, Christians were melted and broken before God, resulting in a renewal of zeal and deeper fellowship between believers. The spread of the revival to Uganda is undoubtedly one of the secrets behind the survival of the Ugandan church under the suffering of the terrible regime of Idi Amin after his coup in 1971. Bishop Festo Kivengere relates the impact that the revival made upon him. 'It came,' he said, 'first, to our rather dead church, when I was a schoolboy in 1935. We listened in amazement . . . never before had we seen such glowing faces. Almost no one responded during these meetings. We were too unfamiliar with the truth and scared by exposure to it. But during the next month many things happened. Schoolboys went to the headmaster, weeping, to return stolen books and to confess breaking the rules. Lives were changed all around us. People saw visions and dreamed dreams. So many repented that pagans were afraid to walk up our hill for fear that God would lay hold of them. The fire of God spread and congregations came alive spiritually.[3]

Repentance and confession paved the way for the Spirit of God to work. The Korean revival (or, as it is usually known, the Korean Pentecost) started as a result of the 1904 Welsh revival. News of what had happened in Wales came to Korea, and as a result a group of Presbyterian ministers got together to pray for revival. In August 1906 they met for a week of prayer and Bible study. They had a deep concern for the need of the country in the time in which they lived. At the New Year, 1,500 men gathered together. So many of them wanted to pray that the leader told everybody, 'If you want to pray—all of you, pray together!' Simultaneous audible prayer became a feature of church life in Korea, and is practised today in many parts of the church worldwide.

A tide began to sweep through the church. There was no confusion, it was a single harmony of prayer as if voices of all the praying congregation merged together to form a single cry to God. The Holy Ghost welded them all together into one. At this great prayer meeting one worshipper after another rose, confessed his sin then fell to his knees again, weeping and begging God for forgiveness.[4]

It was not just a confession of sin to God; it was an audible confession in front of other people. The meeting went on for days, with confession, weeping and trembling. The heathen were astounded. Delegates to the New Year gathering of churches carried the revival to their various churches—to the people of God, not to the outsiders. The results were always the same wherever they carried the revival: deep conviction of sin, followed by confession and restitution, together with the new feature—audible prayer in unison.

Rene Monod, who was highly sceptical both of the

possibility that God might be moving and of the simultaneous prayer meetings, nevertheless radically changed
his views when, as a missionary in Korea, he saw God
working miracles.

> Deadly enemies made their peace with one another, stolen
> money and goods were returned, past injustices were set
> right, not only between Christians but to pagans as well. One
> old Chinese business man was much surprised when a
> Christian returned to pay a sum of money which he had once
> received from the merchant in error. Many heathens were
> converted and brought to Christ by the honourable conduct
> of these Christians.[5]

If we hold on to things in our lives that are wrong, we
not only block ourselves off from the full blessing of God
and his Son as delivered at Pentecost; we also block
others from receiving the forgiveness and love of God.
If we could humble ourselves and admit our faults
and failings—and we all have them—it would be a major
step towards binding us together in acceptance and
unity.

God wants to change society

Secondly, God does not only express his holiness in
revival to individuals. It is his purpose to bring about
radical change in a decadent era. As we have seen,
when God's Spirit is outpoured, society is always
affected. But as we allow God to change us as people,
we ourselves become the agents of change in society. He
works through his people. And the cumulative effect of
many individuals being changed is that society feels the
impact.

We see this phenomenon in many of the Old Testament
accounts of spiritual revival. In Hezekiah's day, for
example, we see a progression. First Hezekiah did what
was right before God. Then he called the priests and

Levites together. Their first task was to clear the rubbish out of the temple and make it fit for worship once more. But, before that, they consecrated themselves. At the first worship service, however, not enough priests were consecrated, so others had to be made holy. Next, an edict was issued to the people of Israel to come and return to the Lord. As the large crowd gathered in Jerusalem, there were tokens of heart-response; both in relation to God (in that more were consecrated), and in relation to the world (in that they cleared away the false altars). After the festival, they tackled with zeal the task of purifying the land's towns and cities from idolatry (see 2 Chronicles 29–31).

In the early 1970s, there was a revival in Saskatchewan in Canada. Churches were jammed to capacity. Thousands were being converted to Christ. And one of the features of that revival was that Christians were going to shopkeepers to return goods they had stolen, and to people they had defrauded to put things right. People were making restitution, and long-standing sins were dealt with honestly.

Some time ago, I met a man named Jack. He was converted in Bristol during the 'Teddy boy' era. One of the first things he was convicted about after his conversion was his home. 'Every stick of furniture in my home was stolen,' he told me. 'I had to take everything back to the place I'd stolen it from. For a while my wife and I ate off an upturned tea-chest in the front room. It was the only thing left on the floor.' That was real restitution! It took honesty to carry through the holiness of God into everyday life, despite the consequences.

In revival crime falls, social change takes place and a sense of corporate holiness follows.

The Welsh revival produced a social awakening.

Long standing debts were repaid and stolen goods returned. In Maesteg a tradesman received a live pig in payment of a debt that had been outstanding since 1898. Magistrates in several places were presented with white gloves, signifying there were absolutely no cases to try.[6]

Life in the mines was transformed. Not only did workers and management engage in prayer meetings, but they had texts chalked on ventilating doors for all to see. Cursing and profanity were so diminished that pit ponies could not do their work—they hadn't yet learned the new language of Zion! Wherever the revival spread in Wales the results were the same—the quickening of church members, the conversion of outsiders and the virtual elimination of drunkenness and swearing. All feuds inherited from a bitter strike were settled.

Britain's Social Services are stretched to breaking point. So are the Health Services and the criminal departments. Sin is breaking loose among young and old alike. There is a horrific incidence of child abuse, child prostitution and drug addiction. The decline of family life is reaching tragic proportions; nearly half of all marriages now end in divorce. In 90% of single-parent families, the single parent is the mother, so many children are deprived of a father, and when we talk about the love of our heavenly Father, they have nothing to compare it with.

But I believe that when God does move by his Spirit, we shall see a reaffirmation of the family as the essential basic unit for a stable society. A rediscovery of harmony in the home will inevitably lead to a rapid reduction in many social ills.

We shall expect to see God move by his Spirit to change society when he comes with his holy character. The expression of God's holiness will be to the community as well as to the individual.

God wants to change the church

Some of us will find this concept the most difficult. We can envisage God supernaturally changing society. We can recognise that he can change us as individuals. But when we look at some churches, we may well shake our heads and wonder: Can it happen? Supernatural manifestations are always associated with the movement of God's Spirit in times of spiritual awakening. Yet some churches and some church leaders are frightened of what God might do, unbelieving about what he can do, and unwilling for what he wants to do.

Many like to keep within 'denominational tramlines'. They do not accept that God can actually work in other denominations. Yet one of the distinguishing marks of the 1859 revival, for example, was the fact that God worked in all the denominations. In America the Baptists had so many converts that they had to cut a hole in the ice to baptise the thousands! As Edwin Orr has remarked, 'When the Baptists do that, they really are on fire!'

Some people feel threatened by the unpredictable, supernatural working of God—'Things might get out of control!' But whose control are they talking about? God's—or man's? God *does* want to change the church. There needs to be an essential sense of unity among the body of Christ, and in revival God creates a sense of unity that wasn't there before. We need to be prepared for that. We need to pray for it, and we need to be ready for God's power first to be exercised in the house of God: 'It is time for judgment to begin with the family of God; and if it begins with us, what will the outcome be for those who do not obey the gospel of God?' (1 Pet 4:17).

God wants to begin with us. Are we ready for it?

What do you do about the things that are wrong in your church? Do you criticise the leadership? Do you talk with one another behind closed doors about the church's ills? Or do you pray?

God is *interested* in the church. He's the Head of it. It's what he brought into being; it's his. That's why one of the Enemy's strategies is to attack the church of Jesus Christ. If he can separate us from the Godhead so that we are not looking to Jesus Christ the Head of the church, but to subsidiary heads—mere men with feet of clay—for our leadership, he's done his job. If he can get us criticising the Head, even denying the deity of Christ or the relevance of the Holy Spirit in our congregations, then Satan has succeeded.

There is nothing so potent as a congregation of revived Christians; people who are actively sharing the love of God between themselves and who also move out in caring relationships with others who are outside the family of God. When the holy character of God is seen to be present and resident in that congregation, people are attracted. In revival times a congregation displaying the love and holiness of God became so vibrant that sometimes people were almost propelled into their services, as if by some invisible hand.

The early church at Jerusalem was such a church. They devoted themselves to the Lord and to each other; God moved miraculously with signs and wonders; they shared their possessions and there was no needy person among them. When a married couple decided to deviate from what God was doing among them, the honesty and holiness of God and his people was threatened. So the word of knowledge from God, through Peter, to Ananias and Sapphira, brought an awesome end to that act of deceit. The church was characterised by power.

Common denominators of changed churches

When churches change, the nature of the change varies. It depends on what neglected truth God sovereignly causes to be rediscovered. But certain common denominators can be identified.

One is *unity*. Different congregations of God's people discover each other. Feuds are resolved. Fears are overcome. Wounds are brought into the open. Christ's love binds people together, and God does a deep work in restoring relationships and recreating fellowship.

Evangelism is another. It ought to be the emphasis of every local church, but because of human weakness, failure and timidity, all too often it isn't. But in an awakening, evangelism happens spontaneously. God is at work, and he moves out into the world. Otherwise, his reviving work within the church would quickly stagnate. Revival has to be spread and shared; it can't be confined or shut up.

But it is *distress over sin* and a desire to be radically different that seem to characterise most movements of God's Spirit. In accounts of revival in Northampton New England in 1740–42, in narratives of the Welsh revival of 1904–5, and in later accounts nearer our own time, we read of conviction of sin in a congregation being so genuine that it resulted in many tears. There were voices crying out to God for forgiveness and mercy, public confessions of sin, even faintings and 'prostrations'. Jonathan Edwards described how some were prostrated for twenty-four hours—'with their senses locked up; but in the meantime under strong imaginations, as though they went to heaven and had there a vision of glorious and delightful objects.'[7]

In the Welsh revival, church services seemed to have little structure once the Spirit of God started to move. There would be singing, testimony, exhortations, spontaneous and even simultaneous audible prayer. Sometimes Evan Roberts attended services but did not preach —he let the Spirit of God do his work. There also seemed to be no set time for services to end. In revival times it is common for services to last well into the night (one service recalled by William Haslam in his autobiography *From Death to Life* lasted eight days non-stop). A friend of mine who was ministering in a revival area on the Island of Borneo in South-East Asia told me that services used to start at 5 am before daybreak and continue until midnight. He used to sleep on the platform while his colleagues preached. They woke him when it was his turn to take over!

It appears that some churches in an area of revival missed out on what God was doing, because they were unwilling to change, or because of their criticisms or suspicions of what was happening elsewhere. Haslam described how he was unwelcome in many churches because they were suspicious about the manifestations of God's power in the Cornish revival of the 1850s. He was criticised by high churchmen and by legalists. He observed that more were concerned to defend the truth than to proclaim it. Many were more interested in building their own congregation or kingdom than in extending Christ's kingdom. 'Where the church was rising up into energetic action, in too many cases it had a sectarian object—that is, they were trying to make churchmen or communicants, and not proclaim the Gospel of Christ.'[8]

When God moves in his church he deals with hypocrisy and heresy. Both are aberrations of truth and can't easily exist in a genuine revival. So the false, the humanistic, the self-congratulatory ego-centred expressions that pass for Christianity will seem shallow and superficial alongside the real thing. He also deals with lethargy, loose living and double standards. If those are present in the church as a general sickness, they will prevent the movement of God's Spirit to any degree, unless they are repented of.

God wants a holy church 'cleansing her by the washing

with water through the word, and to present her to himself as a radiant church, without stain or wrinkle or any other blemish, but holy and blameless' (Eph 5:26–27). Here is the same sense of holiness as being 'morally blameless, physically pure and ceremonially clean'. God wills that to happen in revival since he wants to work through a beautiful church and not a tarnished one. 'The church must first repent, then the world will break! The church must first weep, then our altars will be filled with weeping penitents.'[9]

In the letters to the seven churches in Revelation chapters 2 and 3, the Head of the church spoke about their need. He had complimentary things to say, but he also had uncomplimentary things. He warned five of the churches about the influence of Satan. To one: 'You've got the synagogue of Satan.' To another: 'You've got the seat of Satan here; this is where Satan sat.' He warned another about Jezebel and her influence, and the way in which people were going after sexual idolatry of one kind and another.

Today, those churches, apart from Smyrna, have disappeared. Islam has taken over. Where they once existed is now one of the most anti-Christian parts of the whole world.

What would he say to compliment or criticise our local church today? What is the Spirit saying to the church? And are we hearing his voice and responding in obedience? For that is essential if we want to see God's power released. God wants his world back, and holiness in the church is his chosen method.

Notes

1. Duncan Campbell, *The Price and Power of Revival* (Faith Mission), pp 51–52.
2. J Edwin Orr, *The Flaming Tongue* (Moody, 1973), p 20.

3. Colin Whittaker, *Great Revivals* (Marshall Pickering, 1984) pp 118–119.
4. *ibid*, p 140.
5. Rene Monod, *The Korean Revival* (Hodder & Stoughton, 1971).
6. J Edwin Orr, *op cit*, pp 18–19, 12.
7. Jonathan Edwards, *Jonathan Edwards on Revival* (Banner of Truth) p 154.
8. William Haslam, *From Death to Life* (Good News Crusade, 1976), p 197.
9. Leonard Ravenhill, *Why Revival Tarries* (STL Trust, 1972), p 75.

7

Awareness of Sin

Who may ascend the hill of the Lord? Who may stand in his holy place? He who has clean hands and a pure heart, who does not lift up his soul to an idol or swear by what is false. He will receive blessing from the Lord (Ps 24:3–5).

We saw in Chapter five that it was the impact of these verses that struck to the hearts and consciences of those who prayed all night in a Hebridean barn in 1949, just before revival came.

The significance wasn't so much the verse itself, nor the version of the Bible being used. It was simply that a few people were prepared to take God at his word. They linked the promise with the condition. To receive blessing, by standing in the Lord's holy place, is something reserved for those who are prepared to say in complete honesty that so far as they know they are pure, true and single-minded in their worship of God. The Hebridean group were utterly sincere; there was no hypocrisy in their coming before God. They had no double standards to keep them guilt-ridden. There was no condemnation for them from the scripture, 'These people come near to me with their mouth and honour me with their lips, but their hearts are far from me' (Is 29:13; Mt 15:8–9).

The late Bishop Festo Kivengere, speaking of the East African revival, remarked in my hearing, 'Unless God does something under *my* buttons, I will not see it under the buttons of someone else!' In the Hebridean revival, people similarly looked first at themselves. Awareness and confession of sin became a bridge to fellowship. Confession was not just a biblically endorsed practice (eg Jas 5:16). They were prepared to put into practice what God had spoken to them individually.

Our Western version of Christianity has conditioned us to exposition, to daily Bible reading notes and to sermons, yet often the word of God doesn't mean as much to us as it once did. In our heads we acknowledge the truth of what we read, but we don't let it drop into our hearts. Some of us have such an intellectual faith that we treat sermons and Christian literature as if they were works of art and we were the critics. As a result, the value we place on them has more to do with our preconceptions and theological assumptions than with anything God may actually have said to us personally.

Many people sense that God is challenging them through the authority, power or anointing of his word, but they let the moment pass, and content themselves with condescending compliments to the preacher: 'I did enjoy your sermon'—or book, or whatever. The word of God, spoken *to them*, is not received with faith and obedience, so it never becomes the liberating word it was meant to be.

I was once washing dishes with an evangelist's son. We had just returned from a meeting at which I had been preaching. It was one of those times when I had been conscious of the anointing of God. I had preached my heart out! So I asked him how he had received what God had been saying that night. I wasn't looking for bouquets. I was simply interested to know the response of a keen young Christian. But to my astonishment, he told me that he couldn't remember a word I'd said. I asked him why. He confessed, 'I suppose I've become so used to hearing sermons that I switch off now when the preacher begins.'

I wonder, how many in our congregations are like that? So many must be missing God by 'switching off'! And when God *does* get hold of a man or woman and they begin to do exploits in his name, the personality cult often takes over, and they are put on a pedestal built by the 'word of testimony' and articles in the popular Christian press.

Sometimes it's as if we put people on pedestals to escape the obligation of following their example. We don't want to obey God's call, so we make them into heroes, and of course we can't be expected to be like them.

And yet people who are blessed by God, who are used in revival, aren't superhuman heroes or extraordinary personalities. They are people who have been prepared to be honest with God, with others and with themselves.

Examining ourselves

What would happen if we were prepared to take the words of Psalm 24 seriously? What if, in total honesty, we asked God to scrutinise us by his Spirit? What if we were willing to take action on whatever God may say to us, not just as a spontaneous response, but also as a continuing process? Wouldn't we then begin to see reality dawning in our Christian lives?

Or what if we took for ourselves God's word to Solomon, and humbled ourselves, sought his face, turned from our wicked ways and prayed (2 Chron 7:14)? Would we not find that God is equal to his promises?

If with the same sincerity we prayed the Evan Roberts prayer of the Welsh revival—'Lord, bend us, bend me'—and were prepared to have the humility and submission to God's will that that prayer implies, would we not be available channels for the power of God?

That power is greater than ours could ever be, and the reason is that the channels through which it flows are willing to show that 'the all-surpassing power is from God and not from us'. The more we concentrate on our own reputations, or the welfare of our particular organisation, the less likely we are to become such willing channels. As Nick Cuthbert remarks:

> When Christians in this country start unitedly to cry to God to save the lost, without an eye on their own personal shrine, and not minding how He does it or through whom, then we shall see the power of God released ... the Lord will not allow anybody to build their own empire in the name of the kingdom of God.

Awareness of sin is always associated with periods when God is working in a special way. In times of 'enhanced spirituality' such as conventions or Bible weeks, we often become much more acutely aware of personal failing. Things that we may never have identified as offensive to God are exposed in the general climate of spiritual truth into which we have temporarily placed ourselves. When that climate pervades a period of time or a geographical region—which is what happens in revival—our awareness of personal sins becomes more and more intense, and a desire to be clean and to put right the things that are wrong follows.

How the Spirit deals with sin

I can think back to times in my own life when God has confronted me in this way with specific things that needed to be put right. Particularly significant to me was my own renewal experience in 1978. Not long after God invaded my life with fresh joy and delight, he began to confront me with specifics.

In the first week of my 'renewal state' I was often overwhelmed with the joy and reality of Christ's presence. It was so real that it sometimes seemed physical. It didn't matter where I was, he was there and wanted to share something with me. But at the same time I became acutely aware of anything that seemed the slightest turning away from him. It might be a wrong thought, a hasty word, an improper action—and it was almost as if the physical presence of Christ was at once withdrawn. 'Don't go, Lord!' I cried. 'I'm sorry to have offended you. Please forgive me and cleanse me now—and do come back.' Whereupon there was an immediate *awareness* (not just a theological assumption derived from 1 John 1:9) that he had come back.

Later, as I prayed to God to bless my wife in the same way, I began to realise that the Spirit was telling me that there were things wrong in my relationship with her, things in my habits and conduct and attitudes that needed to be put right. I had to confess to her particular things by which I had soured our relationship—things she had never known about. That process wasn't something I would have been naturally inclined to go through! But because God was doing the necessary spiritual surgery, and because I intensely desired to walk in step with him, I obeyed. And as a result, not only was the way opened for my wife to receive rich blessing from the Lord, but a closeness and unity began in our marriage which we hadn't known before.

If we are to receive 'times of refreshing' from the Lord (Acts 3:19), sins have to be 'wiped out'.

Acts 3:19 was originally spoken to people who had seen a miracle. We can assume that they weren't believers in Christ at the time, though they may have been familiar with the concept of repentance. So if their repentance, and the wiping out of their sins that followed, would produce such times of refreshing for them—how much more should it do so when God's people, those who already believe, do the same!

Which comes first: the repenting and blotting out of sins, or the 'times of refreshing'? Usually the former. But times of refreshing always lead to an awareness of sin and a turning away from it as a result. The presence of God produces the awareness; his holy character exposes the faults. Because he is there, we no longer have a cloak. The all-pervading light and reality of Christ shows every speck of dirt, like the sunlight suddenly allowed to stream into a room when the curtains are pulled back, and insects accustomed to nooks and crannies suddenly scurry away from the bright rays.

J I Packer described revival like this: 'We are like sleepers shaken awake and half-blinded by the sudden invasion of light and the unaccustomed glare. We see things as we never saw them before.'

There are two ways in which awareness of sin comes during a revival. First, there is the Spirit's exposure of sin, which we have just described, working in individuals and groups. Secondly, there is the general climate of 'God-consciousness' that is all around during a revival, maintaining people in an awakened state by exposing sin as and when it is committed. The first process produces awareness of sin; the second sustains it.

During the Welsh revival, a young man told Evan Roberts how he had called on every house in a certain street:

The Welsh prophet fixed his piercing gaze upon him and contradicted him. The young man stammered in confusion and admitted that he had not performed all that he had claimed. He trembled like a leaf and burst into tears when Evan Roberts told him that his deceitful ways had followed his forging of a signature on an earlier occasion.[1]

What then are the sins of which God may want to make us aware today as a preparation for an outpouring of blessing?

1. The sin of silence

First, the sin of silence—sin in the face of the world's spiritual, moral and social need.

We who are Christians have kept silent as standards have deteriorated. We've remained silent, and secularists and humanists have had their say. We've held our tongues while occult influence, Satan-worship and witchcraft have increased, while all sorts of fringe activities such as tarot cards, palmistry and astrology have entered the mainstream. Other religions, cults and all manner of New Age groups have increased their influence and their membership. Social evils such as unemployment, racism, addiction and the breakdown of family life have mushroomed. Violence, rape, physical abuse and sexual abuse are escalating.

Appalling human need confronts us on our television screens every day, and we have either gaped like ghouls, or have retreated into our pet forms of escapism. Our complacency has led to a lack of compassion and a failure of nerve.

How do we deal with our silence? By confessing our sin to God by presenting him with our bodies, minds, wills and tongues. And by asking him to give us boldness (see Acts 4:29) and the opportunity to speak for him on issues that matter, so his name is honoured rather than dishonoured.

2. *The sin of fear*

We have lost our nerve. We've been paralysed by fear; fear of what others might think, fear of losing friendships, fear of being misunderstood, fear of the unknown.

Many people who have become Christians have grown up in an atmosphere of rejection. They hesitate to commit themselves to any action or statement that would lead to disapproval or rejection. Consequently fear of being hurt paralyses them and they cannot make in-depth relationships.

Similarly, fear of being dismissed can sometimes lead a Christian into compromising work practices or business decisions; when our livelihood is threatened, we are more tempted to comply with what is expected of us.

There are many other fears that overwhelm people. For example, fear of the future in a nuclear age, and fear of the present in a world where many are lonely.

Many of us are afraid of doing anything that might upset the theological apple cart, that might disturb the status quo in the structures of Christian leadership, or might simply interrupt the peace and quiet of how things are. So we are seized by inertia.

Where does our fear come from?

It comes from the pit. 'God has not given us a spirit of fear'—so it must be the Enemy who has not only planted the seed, but has watered it well by his destructive and manipulative suggestions.

How do we overcome it?

By allowing the love which God has for us to invade our vulnerable areas and our weaknesses, so that we are much more conscious of love flowing through us and overflowing to others than we are of our fears. 'There is no fear in love. But perfect love drives out fear, because fear has to do with punishment' (1 Jn 4:18).

3. The sin of guilt

Awareness of sin always produces an initial burden of guilt, but when God's remedy of grace is made available to us and received by us, the burden lifts.

Yet many of us continue to carry that burden of guilt, and until it is taken from us and we experience release, the weight of it will effectively block revival.

The burden can take various forms. Some are painfully easy to identify. The guilt to do with being the perpetrator or the victim of sex sins and abuse; of homosexual or lesbian practices; of pre-, extra-, or non-marital sexual relationships; of shady business dealings, pilfering, dishonesty, habitual deceit; of one's past life. Richard Foster and the late Bishop Festo Kivengere both identified similar areas which cause many Christians great problems. Richard Foster's book *Money, Sex and Power*[2] cites these three things as the major obstacles to personal discipleship. Festo Kivengere has said that 'money, sex and pet doctrines are the last blocks to be removed'.

Some guilt is far subtler. We can feel guilty because of our failures: our failure to pray enough, to read the Bible enough, to witness enough (though that begs a question: How much is 'enough'?). There can be guilt because we feel we have failed to achieve what was expected of us, that we have failed in our marriage relationships, that our ministry is a failure, and our conviction that it must be our fault is reinforced when we see other people succeeding in those very areas.

Whatever the cause, we retreat into despair and defeatism. Our self-image is badly dented. We go into a spiral of ineffectiveness and despair.

And yet, however guilt is produced in us—whether it be by a critical spirit, hatred, pessimism, unbelief, idolising tradition, or compromise about money, sex or power—there is a way out.

We must go to the cross and become re-awakened.

'Surely he took up our infirmities and carried our sor-
rows ... But he was pierced for our transgressions ...
The Lord has laid on him the iniquity of us all ... He
bore the sin of many, and made intercession for the
transgressors' (Is 53:4–6, 12). 'If we confess our sins, he is
faithful and just and will forgive us our sins and purify us'
(1 Jn 1:9).

I long to see a people of God who are living harmoniously with Christ. A people without a burden of guilt
and fear. A people who are released in spirit, so that mind
and tongue are also released. A people who have discovered that sin is no longer a problem to them.

That does not mean that they don't encounter sin and
temptation. We will all continue to do so. But when
we've got through the guilt barrier and are secure in God,
we won't be aware of sin as a constant burden and
problem. The sins we *will* be aware of will be those we
find ourselves doing every day, and for which we daily
seek God's grace to triumph and live victoriously and
dangerously. But the sins of yesterday will be forgiven
and forgotten.

When we arrive at that state we can truly be revived
Christians—even if we are not yet living in a climate of
general revival. We don't have to wait for revival to come
before we can be revived Christians.

Throw off what hampers your service, even though it be
venerable with the history of ages, or consecrated by dear
familiarity. Use these things as aids to service if you can, but
if they are only clogs cut them off and cast them from you.
The day is come that burns like fire for Christ has cast His fire
on earth. Come out from your safety and comfort, come out
from your habits and conventions, listen for the voice of the
wind as it sweeps over the world and stand where you may be
caught in its onward rush.[3]

Notes

1. J Edwin Orr, *The Flaming Tongue* (Moody, 1973),
   p 21.
2. Richard Foster, *Money, Sex and Power* (Hodder &
   Stoughton).
3. Archbishop William Temple.

8

Come Back, Go, Convert and Sing

One of the characteristics of revival is that as Christians are woken up from their lethargy, many important truths concerning doctrine and the life of the church are rediscovered. Perhaps they have not exactly lain dormant, but neither have they been properly emphasised. But in revival, the Spirit of God brings to the fore what has been allowed to fall into the background.

We have seen already that people caught up in a spiritual awakening are very conscious of the presence of God. Instead of taking it for granted, or assuming God to be present because of the emphasis of some proof texts or a theoretical understanding of the 'indwelling of the Holy Spirit'—suddenly God's people *know* that they are God's people, because they *know* that he is among them.

We have also seen how the Holy Spirit communicates a sense of the holiness of God. Instead of casually tolerating sins, wrong attitudes and wrong behaviour, people are stung by the realisation of their own guilt and need for cleansing. God's holiness is no longer something which only has to do with personal pietism. It affects their actions in the community, as the crime rate falls, immorality declines, stolen goods are returned and swearing stops.

After the initial impact of God's holiness comes awareness of sin. How often we tend to make excuses for the misdeeds we do every day. But what previously seemed of little significance becomes, after revival, extremely significant. The little indiscretions, the white lies, the moments of laziness, the unspoken yet hurtful thoughts —these things, and more, interrupt our fellowship with God and make us instantly aware that we need to confess our sins and seek the renewal of the presence of God which seems, for a while at least, to have been withdrawn.

The picture would not be complete without at least a brief consideration of other marks of the Spirit's visitation. If we look at that first occasion in the Acts of the Apostles, we find evangelism, a call to overseas mission and a conviction that Christ's return was imminent.

Evangelism

Some people hope that evangelism can help to bring about revival. The elements usually found in successful evangelism—such as prayer, repentance, faith and new life—are also usually found in a spiritual awakening. Some people subscribe to Finney's view that revival is 'the right use of the appropriate means'. There is evidence to support this view, though it usually relates to local experiences rather than to geographically extensive revivals.

Tommy Hicks was a forty-four-year-old American evangelist who had a remarkable vision, in which God made it plain that he wanted him to go and preach the gospel in Argentina. He knew so little about the country that when the name 'Peron' kept coming into his mind, he had to ask an air hostess whether she knew anybody of that name. When he discovered that Peron was the

President, it did not shake his conviction that this was the man God wanted him to find.

He set out to obtain an audience with Peron, and reached the office of the minister of religion, whose secretary came in limping with an injured leg. Hicks prayed for him and he was instantly healed, whereupon Peron granted him an audience.

The result was that Hicks was given every encouragement on his mission to preach the gospel. He was offered the use of a large football stadium, and the free use of the Government radio and the press. So he began to preach. He preached for fifty-two days, with an aggregate audience of two million.

Historians have described the Hicks campaign of 1954 as 'a sovereign breakthrough of God'. His meetings broke the back of the entrenched resistance to the gospel. Only 20,000 people made a public response to the preaching of the gospel in the stadium, which was a low figure compared with many other evangelistic crusades elsewhere; yet the campaign made a profound impact upon Argentina.

A spiritual revival such as we have just described is not a *guaranteed* result of evangelism. But the reverse is certainly true: while evangelism doesn't necessarily generate revival, revival *always* generates evangelism. Colin Urqhart has said: 'A revival among God's people results in a great move of evangelism among the lost. He gives His children deep heart-concern for those condemned to a Christless eternity, unless they respond to the gospel of the Kingdom of Heaven.'[1]

Orr's definition of revival is that 'the outpouring of the Spirit effects that reviving of the church, the awakening of the masses, and the movements of uninstructed people towards the Christian faith: the revived church, by many or by few, is moved to engage in evangelism, in teaching and in social action.'

An article in the *Alliance Witness* some years ago described the effects of the revival in Canada in the early 1970s. Describing a campaign that had been in progress for thirty-one days, the author wrote:

> It defies explanation on a merely psychological or natural level. No efforts were made to publicise the meetings. Music of any kind was minimal. Several nights there was no preaching. The Sutera twins made no attempt to promote themselves. They were more like stagehands than leading actors in the drama of the Saskatoon revival. The schedule was gruelling. Services ran for three hours or more and the 'afterglow' sessions sometimes lasted until four or five in the morning. Participants lost all sense of time as one day telescoped into another ... Believers were witnessing to the unconverted. Christians were sharing their experiences with one another. It was a deep work of God that did not stop with the forgiveness of sins and conversion to Christ, wonderful as that peace with God is. It was a revival of love. It closed the generation gap. Estranged husbands and wives, radiant in their newfound joy, were like newlyweds. Sisters long out of fellowship embraced each other with tears of joy. A mother of three children testified with a holy glow on her countenance that God had given her love for the woman who robbed her of her husband. It was a revival that loosed reluctant tongues. Timid people who 'couldn't have been paid to stand up before a group' were testifying fearlessly and honestly before 1,800 in the city's largest church.

In every revival there is a surge outwards, as the revived church communicates with fresh fervour and renewed faith the unchanging (but life-changing) message of the gospel. Young children who have been Christians only for days share their faith. Long-established Christians find new freedom and boldness witnessing for Christ. As Orr said, 'In times of revival, the whole church engages in evangelism, while able evangelists are recruited by the Spirit for a lifetime of service, as seen from Whitefield to Graham.'

The second Great Awakening is an example. It produced a host of evangelistic initiatives. Moody, one of the world's most renowned evangelists, came to prominence. The CSSM—now part of Scripture Union—was formed in those years.

Edwin Orr himself was used in the revival that swept Brazil. In 1951 he had been in Latin America speaking about what God had done in revivals in the past. As a result, eighty churches in Sao Paulo, Brazil, started weekly prayer meetings for revival. In 1952 he returned, for what turned out to be an eleven-week mission in the city, followed by visits to each of the twenty-five states and territories of Brazil. 'Everywhere the Spirit of God moved; again and again the largest auditorium could not hold the great crowds. Thousands came to Christ as Saviour and Lord. Evening meetings had to be transferred to soccer stadiums.[2]

Observers described this movement during 1952 as 'a crucial hour of victory in the winning of Brazil to Christ'. The Bible Society said: 'Brazil is being shaken by the winds of the Spirit as never before.'

That experience had a profound effect on the future life and ministry of Edwin Orr. Thereafter he devoted himself to recording the 'wonderful works of God'. Whenever or wherever he spoke about revivals past and present, God seemed to move among his hearers. He whetted their appetites and gave them a burden for prayer or a hunger for something similar to happen in their own day and their own country.

I talked to Edwin Orr on many occasions, and from time to time I was privileged to be involved with him in his ministry. So I know how desperately he wanted to get his message across, particularly to evangelists, that revival-generated evangelism was far more effective than man-planned evangelism. Billy Graham has said that if he had his time over again, he would preach less and pray more.

World mission

Another product of revival is a new interest in, and commitment to, world mission. For example, the second Great Awakening gave birth to what we now call 'the modern missionary movement'. It produced pioneers of social reform such as Thomas Barnardo and William Booth, the founder of the Salvation Army. Keir Hardie, the founder of the British Labour Party, was converted under Moody's ministry.

The impetus into world evangelism is particularly to be seen in the lives of two statesmen, H Grattan Guiness and Hudson Taylor (who founded the China Inland Mission, now known as the Overseas Missionary Fellowship). They and their families were deeply committed to world mission. Guiness' daughter married Hudson Taylor's son, and another daughter married the founder of the Sudan United Mission. Guiness himself was a co-founder of the Regions Beyond Missionary Union.

On every continent, the effects of the awakening were shared by newly-called missionaries. Revivals broke out. James Chalmers went to Indonesia, Alexander Duff to India, George Grenfell to the Congo, Mary Slessor to West Africa.

In that period, many interdenominational faith missions were founded. The development of interdenominational co-operation owes much to the second Great Awakening, for this was its lasting fruit. Orr writes:

> There seems no doubt that the whole of the 1859 Revival movement was one great unofficial Evangelical Alliance in itself. The principles of Christian union put forth by the Evangelical Alliance in 1846 (when it was founded), and practised on a world-wide scale in the Awakening of 1858–1860, conditioned Christians the world over for the great interdenominational Councils of the 20th century.[3]

The Evangelical Alliance influenced the 1859 revival more by its principles than by its personalities, though most of its leaders were acknowledged as promoters of the awakening. It emphasised the unity of all believers and had a doctrinal basis which became foundational for much of the new work that emerged.

It believed in prayer. A group of missionaries meeting at Ludhiana in North India in 1860 asked the Alliance to extend its 'call to prayer' to the world. It did so. The second week of January was designated a 'Universal Week of Prayer'. The response was phenomenal.

> In areas where the fruits of revival had already been harvested there was a further crop; where the ground was prepared, immediate manifestations of revival sprang up; and where the ground was hard, it was raked and watered by praying Christians for one, two or three years until their prayers were answered in the evangelistic phase of the Awakening.[4]

In the second phase of the second Great Awakening (the early twentieth century) it was not just Wales and England that were affected. In his book *The Flaming Tongue*, Orr shows how the flames of God's supernatural moving were experienced and fanned in Scandinavia, North and Latin America, Australasia, Africa, India, China, Japan and Korea. In almost every case, however, it was spread through messengers who had experienced and shared what God had done.

So the appetites of others were stimulated, and they sought God for themselves, seeking for an outpouring of his Spirit in their locality. Visitors from Norway took the revival back home until Scandinavia was powerfully affected. Welsh missionaries set North-East India ablaze. American missionaries spread the flame in Manchuria and Korea. Many more were converted overseas than were converted in the country where it all began.

Christ issued his Great Commission shortly after his Resurrection. He promised his disciples power before he ascended back to his Father's right hand. But it was not until the Spirit was poured out on the Day of Pentecost that the timid band of believers was equipped to proclaim Christ.

God did his own initial preparation for world mission. People from Mesopotamia, Judea, Cappadocia, Pontus, Asia, Phrygia, Pamphylia, Egypt, Libya, Italy, Crete and from Arab parts heard the wonders of God declared in their own tongues (Acts 2:9–11). Later, a commitment to cross-cultural evangelism was stimulated; first by persecution (Acts 8:1,4), then secondly, through Philip (evangelism to the Samaritans and to the Ethiopian), through Peter (who was told in a vision that the gospel was for Gentiles too), and through Paul on his missionary journeys. Christ gave the Commission, but it was undoubtedly the prompting of the Holy Spirit that brought about its fulfilment.

Can it be that God is today preparing the world for a new outpouring of his Spirit? With today's mass communications, easy travel and multi-racial society, a visitation from God in any of our major cities could have a profound effect throughout the world in a very short space of time. A movement of God in our universities could have a spiritual effect upon future national leaders, and thus upon the nations to which they will return, for generations to come.

Christ's Second Coming

The early church expected the imminent return of Christ. It was an expectation which was not dispelled by such words as those of Jesus in Luke 21:32: 'This generation will certainly not pass away until all these things have happened,' and also: 'This gospel of the kingdom will be preached in the whole world as a testimony to all nations, and then the end will come' (Mt 24:14), nor by the angelic promise in Acts 1:11: 'This same Jesus . . . will come back in the same way you have seen him go into heaven.'

In their preaching, the apostles anticipated Christ's return (see Acts 3:19–20). In the teaching of the epistles, belief in Christ's imminent return was encouraged (2 Pet 3:8–10; Heb 9:28; Phil 3:20; 2 Thess 1:7–10). So too, in times of renewed spiritual vigour, this doctrine is brought into fresh focus.

Revival gives people a touch of heaven. It heightens their awareness of heavenly things, of Christ's promises, of the purpose of existence itself. 'Heaven came down, and glory filled my soul' becomes more than the words of a hymn; it becomes their personal experience. Because revival is concerned with visitation of God's Spirit, and because supernatural and unusual things happen in a revival, people are led to believe that God is ushering in the fulfilment of his purposes. Living in the intensity of what God is doing, in those 'times of refreshing from the presence of the Lord', must make it seem that Jesus is going to return at any moment. Sometimes, people have visions. There are reports of angelic appearances. And the almost physical awareness of God's presence, and the exposure of personal sin before God's holiness, must make it seem that the Second Coming is on the way. And so it is preached.

Orr has said that during the second Great Awakening, 'a preoccupation with the doctrine of the Second Coming arose'. It is stated as a fact, though no documented evidence is given.

Music in worship

It is strange, in view of the importance of music in revival, that we find so few references in the New Testament to singing the praises of God.

There is little evidence that Jesus' disciples were inclined towards singing. Nor is there an emphasis on singing in the accounts of the establishing of the church. It's only when we get to the epistles that we find any references. Paul tells the Romans that the Old Testament describes singing as a characteristic of the Gentiles as they became aware of God (cf Rom 15:11); he encourages the Ephesians to speak to one another with psalms, hymns and spiritual songs (Eph 5:19), and he urges the Colossians to sing to the Lord 'with gratitude in your hearts' (Col 3:16).

Paul's injunctions, however, are in the nature of general teaching on the subject, rather than evidence of widespread practice, though his own testimony is of singing 'with my spirit' and 'with my mind' (1 Cor 14:15). And the Old Testament, of course, is full of evidence of the importance of singing. There are songs from Moses, Deborah, David and the sons of Korah, who were the original musicians in the temple. In the revival in Hezekiah's reign, there was singing and music-making (2 Chron 29:27–30; 30:21). And at the very end of the Bible, we find that there is singing in heaven (Rev 5:9; 14:3).

So it is strange that in the early church there is so little evidence of singing, especially in view of the fact that in most hymn books, the hymns that have the deepest substance are usually the ones written in times of spiritual revival.

The Wesleys were prolific hymn writers: Charles Wesley is said to have written over 6,000 hymns, some of them using tunes from folk songs, opera and the psalter.

Singing—often spontaneous—was a prominent feature of the Welsh revival. Recently a hymn that was known as the 'love-song of the revival' has found new popularity:

> Here is love, vast as the ocean,
> Loving kindness as the flood,

> When the Prince of life, our ransom,
> Shed for us his precious blood . . .

Few English-speaking churches in Wales today are familiar with this hymn, though it is still known in Welsh-speaking areas.

Revivalist preachers of the past two centuries have often been accompanied by musicians. Finney had Thomas Hastings, Moody had Sankey, Torrey had Alexander, and Evan Roberts had his 'singing sisters'.

In the Hebridean revival, psalm singing became a feature as familiar words were set to new music. Today in Britain and North America we are seeing a revival of hymnology and spiritual songs. New material is proliferating, as people express what God has done in their lives, or what he has shown them in Scripture or spoken to them prophetically. Words and music from people like Graham Kendrick and others is surely inspired: short worship songs set to simple music, and majestic hymns, full of spiritual content, are filling modern music books.

The leading of worship is becoming a spiritual art form. Churches are training musicians and using them, producing their own material and compiling their own songbooks. Is this a sign of a new work of God among his people?

Perhaps it is. But we must take care we do not throw away the old songs. The songs of praise are a legacy of happiness that revival leaves behind, enriching the worship of the church in succeeding generations. The Bible points out that when God does a new thing, new songs are sung. 'Sing to the Lord a new song,' says Isaiah, to whom God had said, 'New things I declare' (Is 42:9–13). 'See, I am doing a new thing,' God thunders in the next chapter.

Often flowing prayer and uplifting praise were

intermingled in revival meetings. Sometimes—as in the Welsh revival—not a word was preached.

'Is anyone happy?' asks James. 'Let him sing songs of praise' (Jas 5:13).

The history of revivals illustrates a common pattern. God's people cry out, 'Come Lord Jesus, *come*, quickly.' But God' re-emphasises his desire that his people should go into all the world and *preach* the gospel to every creature. As they go, their hearts are aflame and free, so they express their joy in song, singing and making melody in their hearts to the Lord. God is in his temple; they are on his earth.

They can only go in his strength, with his word on their lips, his Spirit in their hearts and a bit of heaven spread around.

Notes

1. Colin Urquhart, Foreword in: J Oswald Sanders, *The Revival We Need* (Marshall Pickering, 1985).
2. Colin Whittaker, *Great Revivals* (Marshall Pickering, 1984), p 101.
3. J Edwin Orr, *The Second Evangelical Awakening* (Marshall Pickering, 1949), p 218.
4. *ibid*, p 217.

9
Let My People Pray

'Will you not revive us again, that your people may rejoice in you?' (Ps 85:6).

Of all the characteristics of revival, the most important and universally prominent must surely be prayer. In every revival, whether in history or in the recent past, prayer has gone before it, prayer has been a feature of it, and prayer has continued as long as the revival has continued.

Prayer has been the means by which Christians hungry for revival have cried out to a God of mercy. It has also been the means, initiated by God, by which he has told humanity about his intention to take the stage of human history, and by his power, presence and holy character bring to life those who are spiritually dead. Apart from that intervention, many have no other revelation to them on which to base saving faith. Prayer is the means whereby the longing of man and the will of God become one. 'Lasting prayers bring lasting revivals. Prayer does not condition God; prayer conditions us. Prayer does not win God to our view; it reveals God's will to us.'[1]

In my last book, *Three Times Three Equals Twelve* (Kingsway 1986), I wrote in greater detail on the nature of prayer. But in this chapter I want to explore a particular aspect of prayer: revival praying.

There is a difference between praying for revival and revival praying.

Revival praying

When we pray for revival, it may be from a sincere desire to see God move. We may have been praying for years like that, regularly attending revival prayer meetings. But our motives can be very mixed. It can be, for example, a form of escapism: 'If only God would bring a revival, then all our effort wouldn't be needed.' Or it can be a desire to see growth in our own denomination, or even our own ministry. It can even be a selfish motive—'I want revival so that I can say, "I was there," and be in the history books!' In other words, motives can be questionable or they can be genuine reasons for prayer for revival. But they remain merely human reasons.

In revival praying, however, God's glory, power and will become pre-eminent. 'Not to us, O Lord, not to us but to your name be the glory, because of your love and faithfulness' (Ps 115:1).

When we are praying for revival, revival may be just one of several things for which we have a burden—such as evangelism, personal needs, the nation or the next morals-related Bill before Parliament. All these things are very valid things to be praying for, and I would not want to diminish the importance of continuing to pray for such things. But they are short-term issues; they constitute a human agenda, even though in praying for them we are seeking to discern the will of God.

'Prayer for revival is no sudden flight of fancy, no spiritual hobby ... we are not seeking fame, miracles, success, ease, full churches or financial deliverance. These *may* come, but first and foremost we seek the Lord.[2]

In revival praying, however, there is an overwhelming, consuming desire for a visitation from on high. When we give expression to that desire, the Holy Spirit prompts us so that the will of God is uppermost in the praying. A desire for God's glory to be revealed becomes all-consuming—'that his glory may dwell in our land' (Ps 85:9). And we find that God is burdening others to pray similarly, even though they may be few in number. And there is a new desire to spend longer in prayer; even to fast—that is, go without food and sleep, or both—in order to seek him and wait in his presence. We take our place on earth as the angels take their place in heaven, waiting for God's instructions to go into action.

Jonathan Edwards in New England wrote a treatise in response to a plea from a Scottish Presbyterian minister, who called on the people 'of Scotland and elsewhere' to unite in prayer for the revival of religion. Edwards' book was entitled *A Humble Attempt to Promote Explicit Agreement and Visible Union of all God's People in Extraordinary Prayer for the Revival of Religion and the Advancement of Christ's Kingdom on Earth, Pursuant to Scripture Promises and Prophecies Concerning the Last Times*.[3] That lengthy title contains three important phrases: 'explicit agreement', 'visible union' and 'extraordinary prayer'.

Wherever revival praying is happening, all three of these elements will be present to some degree.

Explicit agreement

In the spiritual battle, whether the praying group is the whole army or a reconnoitring platoon, it needs to know what it is expecting to achieve and how it is going to try to achieve it.

'If my people, who are called by my name, will humble themselves and pray and seek my face and turn from their wicked ways ...' (2 Chron 7:14).

When God's people of any nation or generation are led

in 'explicit agreement' by the Spirit—sovereignly, or through a leader—to humility, prayer, seeking God's face and turning from evil, God has promised, 'I will hear . . . forgive their sin . . . and will heal their land.'

In Acts 12 we have an example of 'explicit agreement' in prayer—they were praying to God for Peter in prison (Acts 12:5). Here again was a supernatural and extra-ordinary answer: Peter was brought out by an angel. How often, I wonder, does God use his angels today in responding to the prayers of his people!

Visible union

Revival praying has to be visibly united. It cannot be just a tacit acceptance that we are one because we are 'Christians'. It must be a willingness to unite across barriers in order to seek God. Those barriers, fences, divisions, or disagreements need to be repented of and confessed if that unity is to be real. A paper-over-the-cracks type of unity will not do. The Enemy of the Lord will have too many loopholes if there is no genuine repentance. He will capitalise on doubts, fear, suspicion, anger, hate, critical spirits and gossip. So the prayer that does take place will miss the dimension of 'revival praying', and deteriorate into mere praying for revival.

What are the barriers that divide? Any barriers that can exist within the praying group: denominational differences, age differences, husband and wife disagreements, disputes between two Christians and more. While those barriers are allowed to remain, we will not and cannot be honest in our praying. We will not be able to enter fully into the blessing of God either. What God is looking for is unity of heart and mind.

In *The Korean Pentecost* by William Blair and Bruce Hunt, there are descriptions of deeply emotional scenes of repentance in the Korean revival.

We were aware that bad feeling existed between several of our church officers, especially between a Mr Kang and Mr Kim. Mr Kang confessed his hatred for Mr Kim, Monday night, but Mr Kim was silent. At our noon prayer-meeting on Tuesday, several of us agreed to pray for Mr Kim. I was especially interested because Mr Kang was my assistant in the North Pyengyang Church and Mr Kim an elder in the Central Church, and one of the officers in the Pyengyang Men's Association, of which I was chairman. As the meeting progressed, I could see Mr Kim sitting with the elders behind the pulpit with his head down. Bowing where I sat, I asked God to help him and looking up saw him coming forward.

Holding on to the pulpit, he made his confession. 'I have been guilty of fighting against God. An elder in the church, I have been guilty of hating not only Kang You-moon, but Pang Mok-sa.' Pang Mok-sa is my Korean name. I never had a greater surprise in my life. To think that this man, my associate in the Men's Association, had been hating me without my knowing it! It seems that I had said something to him one day in the hurry of managing a school field-day exercise which gave offence, and he had not been able to forgive me. Turning to me, he said, 'Can you forgive me, can you pray for me?' I stood up and began to pray, 'Apa-ge, Apa-ge' ('Father, Father') and got no further. It seemed as if the roof was lifted from the building and the Spirit of God came down from heaven in a mighty avalanche of power upon us. I fell at Kim's side and wept and prayed as I had never prayed before. My last glimpse of the audience is photographed indelibly on my brain. Some threw themselves full length upon the floor, hundreds stood with arms outstretched toward heaven. Every man forgot every other. Each was face to face with God. I can hear yet that fearful sound of hundreds of men pleading with God for life, for mercy. The cry went out over the city till the heathen were in consternation.

As soon as we were able, we missionaries gathered at the platform and consulted. 'What shall we do? If we let them go on like this some will go crazy.' Yet we dared not interfere. We had prayed to God for an outpouring of his Spirit upon the people and it had come. Separating, we went down and tried to comfort the most distressed, pulling the agonized men to the floor and saying, 'Never mind, brother, if you have sinned God will forgive you. Wait, and an opportunity will be given to speak.'

Finally, Mr Lee started a hymn and quiet was restored during the singing. Then began a meeting the like I had never seen before, nor wish to see again unless in God's sight it is absolutely necessary. Every sin a human being can commit was publicly confessed that night. Pale and trembling with emotion, in agony of mind and body, guilty souls, standing in the white light of that judgement, saw themselves as God saw them. Their sins rose up in all their vileness, till shame and grief and self-loathing took complete possession; pride was driven out, the face of men forgotten. Looking up to heaven, to Jesus whom they had betrayed, they smote themselves and cried out with bitter wailing: 'Lord, Lord, cast us not away forever!' Everything else was forgotten, nothing else mattered. The scorn of men, the penalty of the law, even death itself seemed of small consequence if only God forgave. We may have our theories of the desirability or undesirability of public confession of sin. I have had mine; but I know now that when the Spirit of God falls upon guilty souls, there will be confession, and no power on earth can stop it.[4]

The praying that took place among those Christians was characterised by honesty and openness in confession of sins. The same thing happened in the East African revival. And it is that kind of necessary honesty before God which is a feature of revival praying. It has the element of 'visible union' about it. Which comes first— honesty or prayer? Probably prayer. But as the prayer goes on, the Spirit starts to do his refining work. And it is vital that what he points out as wrong is confessed.

Extraordinary prayer

I would define 'extraordinary prayer' as prayer that isn't sterile and predictable. It is 'extraordinary', because it is not confined to a set time of day or a certain length. It may even be—like the prayer gathering of the Morovians at Herrnhut—unending for 100 years!

It may also be extraordinary because of the *kind* of praying that takes place. In the Korean church in 1907 simultaneous audible prayer became, as we have seen, a new phenomenon. It is still present in the church there today, and also in many other parts of the world.

Prayer is extraordinary when people are oblivious to time, and do not want or need their beds. Prayer is extraordinary when people regularly get up at an early hour. Prayer is extraordinary when God moves in and moves among those who are praying.

Prayer was extraordinary for the early church. They were a praying church before the Day of Pentecost: 'They all joined together constantly in prayer ... they were all together' (Acts 1:14; 2:1). Here was visible union in prayer. In Acts 4, after the release of Peter and John from custody, the Christians 'raised their voices together in prayer to God' (v 24). 'After they prayed, the place where they were meeting was shaken. And they were all filled with the Holy Spirit and spoke the word of God boldly' (v 31). Here was extraordinary prayer—simultaneous audible prayer, a physical shaking, a fresh outpouring of the Spirit.

Duncan Campbell describes an all-night prayer gathering in the Outer Hebrides in 1949, after he had been preaching in a community where 'the opposition was so successful that only seven came near the meetings'.

So we met. There were about thirty of us, and prayer began. I found it a very hard meeting. I found myself battling and getting nowhere as the hours passed. After midnight, between 12 and 1 o'clock in the morning, I turned to a young man in the meeting and said, 'I feel led of God to ask you to pray,' and that dear man rose to his feet and prayed, and in his prayer he uttered words such as I had never heard before. He said, 'Lord, you made a promise, are you going to fulfil it? We believe that you are a covenant keeping God; will you be true to your covenant? You have said that you would pour water on the thirsty and floods upon the dry ground. I do not know how others stand in your presence. I do not know how the ministers stand, but if I know my own heart, I know where I stand, and I tell thee now that I am thirsty, oh, I am thirsty for a manifestation of the Man of thy right hand'—and then he said this—'Lord before I sit down, I want to tell you that your honour is at stake.'

Have you ever prayed like that? Here is a man praying the prayer of faith. I love to believe that angels and archangels were looking over the battlements of glory and saying to one another, 'This is a man who believes God, there is a man who dares to stand solid on the promise of God and take from the throne what the throne has promised.' Believe it, or disbelieve it—and you can verify this if you like—the house shook like a leaf, the dishes rattled on the sideboard, and an elder standing beside me said, 'Mr Campbell, an earth tremor.' I said, 'Yes,' and I pronounced the benediction immediately and walked out to find the community alive with an awareness of God.'[5]

Here was honesty in prayer coupled with the extraordinary; protracted prayer resulting in supernatural manifestations.

The extraordinary nature of prayer in connection with revival sometimes occurs as a prelude to the outpouring of God's Spirit, and always as a feature of it. If prayer—and revival praying, at that, inasmuch as it contains Spirit-prompted desire for God's glory—is a precursor of revival, then, Lord, will you not cause your people to seek you and come to you in sacrificial, 'faith-full' praying?

Prayer as a prelude to revival

In September 1857, a man of prayer, Jeremiah Lanphier, started a prayer meeting in the upper room of the Dutch

Reformed Church Consistory Building, in Manhattan. In response to his advertisement, only six people out of the population of a million showed up. But, the following week, there were fourteen, and then twenty-three, when it was decided to meet every day for prayer. By late winter, they were filling the Dutch Reformed Church, then the Methodist Church on John Street, then Trinity Episcopal Church on Broadway at Wall Street. In February and March of 1858, every church and public hall in downtown New York was filled. Horace Greeley, the famous editor, sent a reporter with horse and buggy racing around the prayer meetings to see how many men were praying: in one hour, he could get to only twelve meetings, but he counted 6,100 men attending. Then a landslide of prayer began, which overflowed to the churches in the evenings. People began to be converted, ten thousand a week in New York City alone. The movement spread throughout New England, the church bells bringing people to prayer at eight in the morning, twelve noon, six in the evening.[6]

A young man of twenty-one, after being in the New York prayer meetings, returned to his home city of Philadelphia and obtained permission to start a prayer meeting in a room during November 1857. After three months, the average attendance was only a dozen people.

If you had experienced revival in New York and come back with a burden for prayer, and after three months you still only had a dozen people coming, wouldn't you think, 'What's the use? It's obviously something for New York and not where I live'? However, in February the meeting place was changed. A month later a wave of revival poured over the city, and soon some 6,000 were meeting every noon for prayer.

In the capital, Washington, five daily prayer meetings were launched, and thousands were attending them. Prayer was at the heart of what was happening throughout the United States at that time. Edwin Orr has said,

'An outpouring of prayer always precedes an outpouring of the Spirit.' And so it proved to be.

For a time it was estimated that not less than 50,000 conversions occurred every week during the winter of 1857–58 in America. The results of the awakening were such that 1,000,000 people were converted out of a population of less than 30 million in the United States of America in the revival in the two–year period, 1858–59. In New York city alone 50,000 had become Christians in the first six months. In certain New England towns 'not a single adult person can be found unconverted.'[7]

That was America. But it was not confined to America. Revival also came to the British Isles. As news of what was happening in America reached Britain, little groups of prayer warriors sprang up throughout the United Kingdom, sparking a sudden surge of intercession. Coming at a time when ministers were confessing how difficult it was to get church members to meetings for prayer, the movement seemed astounding. 'A spirit of prayer is visiting our churches,' said C H Spurgeon. Small prayer meetings grew rapidly; extemporaneous prayer became the outlet of the feelings of the many revived Christians. Revived Christians sought out their unconverted friends and neighbours, and explained the facts of the gospel to them. For years they had allowed their neighbours to pursue their own ways. Suddenly, they felt compelled to witness.

As a consequence one million people were converted in the U.K. during 1860, as 'tongues of fire' descended on rising young evangelists.

Well–known figures, like Lord Shaftesbury, Richard Weaver, Dr Eugene Stock, George Muller, William and Catherine Booth (founders of the Salvation Army) were either involved or were products of the Awakening. Major London theatres were taken over for regular preaching services as churches and cathedrals could not accommodate all who wished to attend. In one winter season, one million people attended those theatres to hear the Gospel. The London response to the Spirit's work was preceded by 200 daily prayer gatherings throughout the capital. Halls were densely packed for nothing but simple prayer for the outpouring of the Holy Spirit.[8]

In more recent times revival occurred in the Philippines during the Marcos regime. For five years, revival was the heart-cry of a core of missionaries in Manila who met weekly for prayer. The Philippines had never known an island-wide revival in all its years of evangelical history. Then a retired pastor, Paul Holsinger, visited the islands. He decided to stay and devote himself to prayer for a nationwide moving of the Spirit.

He and Evangelista Siodora were speakers at a conference in the province of Cotabato. People were facing another crop failure.

Grumbling and discontent were evident among both Christian and non-Christian workers and in sheer desperation the speakers and staff met for prayer one night after the service.

Next morning a great sense of guilt swept over the entire congregation, breaking them down into weeping and confession of sin. Public restitution, private reconciliation and sacrificial giving followed. Scores, and later hundreds, of townspeople were saved there and in neighbouring communities.

God had fulfilled the promise of II Chronicles 7:14. They met his conditions and he met their need—not only in forgiving their sins but in literally 'healing their land'.

Workers who brought reports of the revival back to Far Eastern Bible Institute and Seminary also brought the revival with them. On Thursday, January 15, Pastor Holsinger spoke in chapel and Mr. Siodora led in prayer.

Then a young senior rose to his feet and began to pray. 'Oh God . . .!' he cried. But the words were a groan. He stumbled on. 'In a few months I will be leaving FEBIAS to go forth and preach thy word. And I have no power! I will go back home to face my unsaved family and friends. And, Lord, I have no compassion!'

The prayer was hardly begun when the entire student body bowed low before God in tears. Then student after student sobbed out his sin and failure. Wave upon wave of agonizing conviction washed over hearts. Revival had come.

'It was like the days of Finney,' Pastor Holsinger described it. 'I had preached a sermon and sat down. Another brother led in prayer and sat down. Then suddenly the Spirit fell on those present. It was instantaneous and complete.'

Another likened it to the days of Ananias and Sapphira, recorded in Acts 5. Some who at first caustically resisted the Spirit were smitten down before the Lord. Few left the chapel. For 13 hours the meeting continued. Genuine grief and deep sorrow for sin characterized that entire first day.'[9]

The effect of united prayer upon Christians of all denominations is always the same. Towards God their hearts are stirred with love which must find expression in worship; towards other Christians their hearts are filled with love which finds expression in a Christian unity that transcends the artificial boundaries of race, people, class and creed; towards the outsiders their hearts are filled with love which sets out immediately, like the Good Shepherd, to bring the lost sheep into the fold.[10]

The extraordinary spiritual influences during revivals bring about more results in one week than does a lifetime of labour by dedicated men in ordinary times.

Prayer as part of revival

Extraordinary prayer during the unique work of the Spirit was a particular feature of the Welsh revival in 1904–5 and in subsequent awakenings in India in 1905. The Welsh revival is known as a prayer revival. However, there does not appear to be evidence of agreement, unity or extraordinary prayer *before* God started to work supernaturally.

True, those who were the instruments of revival prayed. Evan Roberts besought God for revival for thirteen years. Seth Joshua and others were also given to much prayer. But the people in the churches were generally not smitten with a sense of revival praying—until the outpouring at Loughor on November 8th, 1904.

On November 11th, the Moriah church was packed to overflowing with 800 or so people. 'Many were on their knees for a long time on account of their distress and agony of soul.' The gathering dispersed at 4.25 am. The next day prayer meetings were held in the homes of the people. A local minister commented that 'the community has been converted into a praying multitude'. At Aberdare the following Monday, 1,000 people crowded Ebenezer chapel. The Tuesday early morning prayer meeting was crowded and lasted four hours, people missing work to pray. At Ammanford, nightly prayer meetings began. Seth Joshua described one that lasted until 2.30 am.

> This has been one of the most remarkable days of my life. Even in the morning a number were led to embrace the Saviour. In the afternoon the blessing fell on scores of young people. The crush was great to get into the chapel. A surging mass filled the temple and crowds were unable to gain entrance. The Holy Spirit was indeed amongst the people.[11]

Bibles were sold out in Ammanford, swearing in the mines gave place to praise, taverns were emptied of rowdy customers.

One of the features of the Welsh revival was simultaneous prayer, which we have already noted. In the revival in Rhos, near Wrexham, there was on November 8th

> simultaneous prayer which overwhelmed preacher and audience. The closing meeting ran from 10 a.m. to 10 p.m. The religious revival was spreading rapidly throughout North Wales beginning in town after town with interdenominational

prayer meetings. There was a quickening of church membership, the conversion of outsiders and the virtual elimination of drunkenness and swearing. In Bangor, crowded congregations would be praying audibly, individually and simultaneously.'[12]

In Pontypridd 1,200 people were on their knees before the Lord praying together simultaneously for the outpouring of the Spirit of God.

The effects of the Welsh revival were not confined to Wales. They spread to many other countries of the world such as Korea and parts of India and Europe, as well as other parts of the British Isles, where similar events took place, and the awakening was also marked by simultaneous audible prayer. In 1905 in Kerala, South India, 17,000 people broke into simultaneous audible prayer at a convention.

The effects of the revival were reported as deep repentance, joy in the Spirit, and a desire to spread the good news. Christians and Hindus were taken up with visions of holy doves and sacred fire. The Hindus who were converted were still standing firm fifty years later. At the same time, at Poonah in East India, schoolgirls were stricken by conviction of sin, and the school became a vast enquiry room for penitents. Conviction was followed by confession.

Alongside the extraordinary emotional accompaniments to these events were physical phenomena: a sensation of burning, simultaneous prayer, speaking with tongues and women praying with loud crying. G H Lang of the Christian Brethren visited Mukti in East India at that time, and commented on something which was quite alien to Brethren practice:

It was a new experience just to hear a thousand women and girls praying aloud at one time. The sound rose and fell like the roar of the sea or the wind in a forest.

The Friends Mission in a place called Hoshangerbad held four days of meetings to intercede for blessing. The visitation came as a 'rushing mighty wind' and within moments hundreds were praying publicly and simultaneously. Miss Evans, a deaf missionary commented, 'Being deaf I rarely hear a prayer, but in the rush of sound I could plainly hear those around me and direct and different each prayer was.'[13]

In Portland, Oregon, USA, 240 major stores closed from 11 am till 2 pm each day to enable people to pray and attend prayer meetings. They signed a mutual agreement that none of them would cheat and stay open. But nobody wanted to go to the stores—they wanted to pray! In Atlantic City there were only fifty adults left unconverted out of a population of 50,000, as a result of that prayer movement.

As we have seen, 1905 was the start of the Korean phenomenon of prayer. But it's still there! It has not died out yet. It's part of the history of the church in Korea, where over half the population are reckoned to be born-again Christians.

It is estimated that every morning around 5 a.m. there are a million Korean Christians in their churches praying. They are praying and working to make Korea a truly Christian nation. They are praying that the flame of revival which God has kindled in Korea will spread throughout Asia and the world. Dr Paul Yonggi Cho whose church has over half a million members said, 'It's not through any special ability on my part, or anyone else's, that this great moving of God has come to this church. However, there is a special secret. The background of prayer is moving the hand of God to direct and anoint the pastor and staff to work in the lives of the congregation.'[14]

In every generation throughout history, revival has come as a result of prayer.

Even as I write this chapter, my spirit is stirred. Do you want to see the power of God released into our nation?

Then you must pray.

Do you want to see God glorifying himself in and through his church?

Then you must pray.

Do you not long for events similar to those I have described, so that all men may know of God and his Christ and be filled with the Spirit?

Then you must pray.

Do you not want to see change in our society—away from the spread of evil, disease, despair, immorality, drug and drink abuse, violence and so on—so that men, women, young people and children are released into liberty, love and life?

Then you must pray.

Casual, occasional, half-hearted, lukewarm, fits-and-starts praying will not do. But burdened, persistent, sacrificial, prolonged, regular—even daily-prayer is needed. 'If my people will humble themselves and pray and seek my face . . . I *will* hear,' God promises. He has promised so much! Enter into the richness of his inheritance.

'Come, let us to the Lord, with contrite hearts return.'

Come, let us seek the Lord! Come, let us pray. Come, let us call on his name and wait in his presence until he visits us again.

Notes

1. Leonard Ravenhill, *Revival Praying* (Bethany House, 1962), p 124.
2. *ibid*, pp 146–147.
3. Quoted by J Edwin Orr in a paper entitled 'The Role of Prayer in Spiritual Awakening'.
4. Transcribed from an original article by William Blair and Bruce Hunt (further details unknown).
5. Duncan Campbell, *The Price and Power of Revival* (Faith Mission), pp 55–56.

6. Paper by J Edwin Orr 'The Role of Prayer in Spiritual Awakening'.
7. J Edwin Orr, *The Second Evangelical Awakening* (Marshall Pickering, 1949), pp 16–26.
8. *ibid*, pp 97–101.
9. Extract from *Moody Monthly*.
10. J Edwin Orr, *The Second Evangelical Awakening* (Marshall Pickering, 1949), p 97.
11. J Edwin Orr, *The Flaming Tongue* (Moody, 1973), p 10.
12. *ibid*, pp 11–12.
13. *ibid*, pp 146–150.
14. Colin Whittaker, *Great Revivals* (Marshall Pickering, 1984), p 147.

10

Spiritual Warfare

Some of my readers may be wondering why we need to work at prayer at all. Why *should* we pray sacrificially, for long periods, with a burden on our hearts? Why even pray at set times? Isn't that just our human pride showing? Aren't we in danger of thinking that it's up to us to convince God that our country needs a revival? After all, God is sovereign! Surely it's his privilege to decide if, when and where revival will come, and who he will use? We can't change that, many would argue. God is all-powerful; he can do what he wants, when he wants.

Well, it *is* true that God does indeed have the power and authority. He knows what he wants to do and when he is going to do it.

But the other side of the coin is that he has chosen to work through his church. That is how God's will is done on earth. And sometimes, he wants to speed up the work of his church. He wants to give some of his 'overflowing grace' to help us achieve more in a short space of time than we could ever do without his supernatural intervention.

Of course Jesus, the Head of the church, is alive in it and in us by his Spirit. But at certain points in history the heavens are opened and God reveals something of his awesome power. There is a parallel to be seen in the incarnation. God sent Jesus into the world and gave him the task of doing his will on earth. But at times the Father intervened: at Jesus' baptism, on the Mount of Transfiguration, at the end of the wilderness temptation and in response to Jesus' prayer: 'Father, glorify your name!' (Jn 12:28).

In the same way, God intervenes for his church which is doing his will on earth, and he intervenes *by means of* his church. And, when he does so, it is in response to the prayers of his people. 'When God intends great mercy for his people, he sets them praying' (Matthew Henry). The praying of God's people ought not to be simply devoted to our own concerns. The Holy Spirit should be involved in our praying. So, if we feel drawn to lengthy, costly prayer, might it not be because the Spirit is prompting us to do so, giving us the deep desire to do so, and the stamina to endure and to cope with disturbed sleep patterns or absence of food? After all, he helps us in our weaknesses, he aids us in our intercession and he groans within us when we are lost for words (Rom 8:26–27).

Revival praying must be Spirit-led praying, Spirit-burdened praying and Spirit-controlled praying. Otherwise it may simply be a human activity, drawing merely upon human strength.

The cosmic battle

However, there is another reason why such praying is necessary. A cosmic battle is being fought. God has legions of angels to do his bidding, but he also has a church on earth to do his bidding. Our obedience in prayer enables the angels to do their task upon the earth. Graham Kendrick's hymn puts it well:

All Heaven waits with bated breath
For saints on earth to pray.
Majestic angels ready stand
With swords of fiery blade.
Astounding power awaits a word
From God's resplendent throne
But God awaits our prayer of faith
That cries 'Your will be done.'

Awake O church arise and pray
Complaining words discard!
The Spirit comes to fill your mouth
With truth his mighty sword.
Go place your feet on Satan's ground
And there proclaim Christ's name;
In step with Heaven's armies march
To conquer and to reign![1]

'We wrestle not against flesh and blood, but against principalities, against powers, against the rulers of the darkness of this world, against spiritual wickedness in high places' (Eph 6:12, AV). So there needs to be an element of warfare in our praying. One skirmish doesn't win a war. There are many battles along the way—and never so many as when praying takes place.

The powers behind the evil that surrounds us must be encountered and overcome in the name of Jesus. Their power has to be challenged and nullified, and their grip on people and geographical areas—even nations—has to be prised away. Satan and his demonic forces will not give way easily where they have been long entrenched.

Daniel prayed and engaged in a partial fast for three weeks before the angel of God broke through the heavenly realms with the answer. The answer was on the way the moment Daniel started praying, but the principality of Persia (where Daniel was at the time) withstood God's angelic messenger for three weeks—until the archangel Michael came alongside as support.

How many of *our* prayers would have beeen answered if we had only persisted? How many times has God intended to come in power, but has been hindered? How many times would he have broken through had his people not stopped praying?

It seems (and it is a real mystery) that God waits for, wants and needs his people to take their place in prayer before he can break through.

> Barriers are not moved by God's omnipotence until the believer takes the initiative and stands his ground in the heavenly places to engage the powers of evil that are directly the cause of ground-level troubles and resists them in the name of the Victor of Calvary.[2]

Crying for help

It's intriguing to see how often in the Bible the intervention of God in human affairs is linked to the cry or prayers of God's people or one of his servants.

Was there not something in the phrase '[Noah] walked with God' (Gen 6:9) that enabled God to intervene?

What took place in the heavenly realms when the Israelites cried out to God from their captivity, and 'God heard their groaning and he remembered his covenant', sending an angel of the Lord to call Moses out of obscurity in the desert to lead the people out of Egypt (Ex 2:23–3:4)?

How long did the Israelites cry to the Lord because of Midian, before he called Gideon (again, through 'the angel of the Lord') to change things (Judg 6:7–12)?

And how many times did various kings of Israel or Judah turn to the Lord in prayer when they faced calamity or crisis, and God heard and reversed situations (eg 2 Chron 20:6–9)?

Again, what of the prayer and ministry of people like Nehemiah, Ezra, Daniel and Jonah? Jonah is a classic example of God's activity. Reluctant though he may have been, the message was eventually declared to Nineveh. It resulted in a decree: ' "Let everyone call urgently on God. Let them give up their evil ways and their violence." ... When God saw what they did and how they turned from their evil ways, he had compassion' (Jon 3:8-10).

'Call to me and I will answer you and tell you great and unsearchable things you do not know' (Jer 33:3). Jeremiah's single message was that God's people should turn from their sin and call upon God; then they would see a change in their circumstances and an end to their captivity (see Jeremiah 29:12–14).

When revival comes

So the cry of God's people reaches God's holy dwelling place. It releases his answer into earthly situations. It counteracts the purposes of Satan, brings relief to captives or captive places, and glorifies God who makes it all possible.

In past revivals the element of spiritual warfare is present, although it is not recorded as such. Today we are acutely aware of the activity of the Evil One—we see so many evidences of how he controls and possesses people's minds, wills and emotions. We learn frequently of Satanist cults and activities. So many Christians are aware of the need for spiritual warfare—even if their knowledge of the nature and practice of it is limited.

We need to learn more. Satan is waging all-out war on the church—seeking to divide it, to distract it or to imitate it by plausible counterfeits. He seems to have more success in dividing and fragmenting Christians than he does in uniting his own side. That's why prayer, and especially united prayer, is so vital if we want to see the internal hurts of the church healed and damage repaired.

To two elderly sisters (both over eighty years old) who prayed in the Outer Hebrides, prayer was conflict. Sitting on either side of the peat fire they prayed through a long winter's night.

> During the last conflict the enemy came leading his demons; but God had promised and we kept him to his word. I lifted my hand, and with the blood of the Redeemer between us and a defeated foe, struck him in the name of the Lord, and he retreated.[3]

The next day they declared to the parish minister: 'Revival has come—send for Mr Campbell.' When he came and started preaching, God broke through. Revival had indeed come.

The elderly sisters, even while doing spiritual battle, pleaded on the basis of one promise of God: 'I will pour water on him that is thirsty, and floods on the dry ground.' They showed they were thirsty.

One inspired saint prayed: 'God, you promised revival; and if you do not send it, how can I trust you again?'

My friend Alan Vincent wrote about revival praying:

> The purpose of our persistence is not to wear down an unwilling God by our importunity, but rather to overcome the stubborn opposition of the hosts of wickedness. Spiritual wrestling with such powers can become very real and at times a far from pleasant experience, but in the end it yields its magnificent rewards.[4].

Revival is sometimes linked with, or followed by, a period of severe persecution. It seems that all hell is let loose against the church, as the Enemy seeks to thwart what God is doing. But he often oversteps the mark, for church history is full of examples of the growth of the church as a result of or alongside persecution.

Canon Bewes, writing in the *World Christian Digest* on

the effects of the East African revival, particularly in Kenya during the Mau Mau uprising, says

> It looks as though God brought all this revival to the Church, because he only knew the time of stress that was coming. After working underground for some time, in 1952 the Mau Mau secret society first startled the world with appalling tales of cruelty and horror. Witchcraft had never died, but it had appeared to be dormant. Now suddenly there was a fusion of modern politics and ancient witchcraft. The Kikuyu had many grievances, but the greatest grievance of all was something vague and imponderable, the pressure of Western civilization. In their revolt against the West, the Kikuyu are not unique, but there has never been anything else quite like Mau Mau, in its insistence on the whole tribe taking the oath, in its violent reversion to paganism, and its brutality—not only towards the white man, but also towards all Kikuyu who would not support it. There were a number of murders of Europeans, but the brunt of the whole attack was borne by the Christian Kikuyu. It is not surprising that many churches were empty, that church elders and teachers were frightened into taking the oath, although often against their will.
>
> And then the wonderful news emerged that although many purely nominal Christians had given way and taken the oath, the Christians in revival, the 'brethren' as they had now come to be called, were standing firm.
>
> One of the clergy was beaten nearly to death because he refused to deny Christ. A hospital nurse was locked up and beaten for three days in an attempt to make her take the Mau Mau oath. A teacher was shot before his pupils because he refused to join in. An evangelist was chopped up, a Christian woman was hanged, and many others were martyred or persecuted because they would neither deny Christ nor help to destroy the Europeans.[5]

The church in Uganda underwent severe trial during the Amin regime. It is still going through fiercely difficult times. Did the revival that the church experienced in the 1950s and 1960s prepare it for what was to happen?

In the Belgian Congo, now Zaire, persecution dogged Christians and many died for their faith at the hands of their oppressors. The revival that came to the Philippines was accompanied by persecution as political forces juggled for position and power.

More recently revival has been experienced in Sabah (Borneo). The Muslim-based party tried to work its way back to power by turning against the growing Christian presence. But the people turned against them and voted for the Christians. They formed the world's only Christian state government in a predominantly Muslim country—that of the Malaysian Federation.

In his book *China Miracle*, Arthur Wallis describes the story of the church in China, and tells how it survived the communist revolution in the 1950s and the cultural revolution in the late 1960s; and how, despite the appalling persecution it suffered, it began to grow again as a few began to pray for several in small secret prayer groups.

> Even while meeting to pray, persecution dogged them. Believers were humiliated, tortured and threatened. Many died in prison, while others were killed or crippled by savage beatings. Ten years later in 1978, there was a powerful move of God's Spirit, with the emergence of house churches throughout China. In one city 50,000 Christians were reported to be meeting in 600 home-based groups—an eighth of the population. Prayer and fasting were 'normal' activities in the villages. In some places there were daily prayer gatherings—and those praying circled the globe in their 'disciplined praying'. And they saw God constantly answer their prayers in miraculous ways—healing the sick, controlling the weather, releasing from demonic powers. This in turn led to the conversion of many in all walks of life.[6]

Persecution is not something any of us seek. When it happens it is painful and costly. Yet biblically it is a way of engaging in spiritual warfare and of overcoming Satan.

When the Book of Revelation pictures the downfall of Satan, it explains that one-third of the angelic throng was cast out of heaven with him (that leaves two-thirds still on God's side, so we always can outnumber the forces of darkness by two to one!). 'There was war in heaven' (Rev 12:7)—Michael against Satan, the dragon or deceiver; both names are used to describe his character. Satan lost and was 'hurled down' to the earth. The nature of his work there is plain: to lead the whole world astray. And he's doing quite well at the present time.

God, however, has not left us at the mercy of all the devil's forces. We are not helpless in the hands of deceiving spirits. We are not to be overwhelmed by the false, insidious accusations that are hurled at us in a variety of forms—criticism, guilt, sarcasm and innuendo, character assassination, low self-worth, fear and so on—and at any time, day or night! And God does not expect us passively to allow him to get on with the job of defeating Satan.

'They overcame him by the blood of the Lamb and by the word of their testimony; they did not love their lives so much as to shrink from death' (Rev 12:11). Three things characterise our means of overcoming Satan's wiles: the blood of Christ, our spoken words of faith and victory, and our willingness to face persecution, even to the point of death if necessary. So persecution and martyrdom can be a means of defeating Satan's purposes, Hallelujah!

Satan sees his role now as 'to make war against . . . those who obey God's commandments and hold to the testimony of Jesus' (Rev 12:17). Please note, his purpose is to 'make war'. It is not merely to distract us, or to irritate us, or even to hurt us, although all those are included.

No, the devil is engaged in all-out war against the church. He uses strategies and tactics; he has demons and evil spirits at his disposal on earth and fallen angels in the 'heavenly realms'; he can 'possess' people and 'oppress' others; he inhabits world systems, cults and the occult. In the next chapter we will examine in a little more detail how he works, and how we can begin to counteract his purposes.

Attacking the devil

Arthur Wallis has said that 'persecution is not aimed at the Church, but at Jesus'. Saul of Tarsus thought he was persecuting the church as he was 'breathing out murderous threats against the Lord's disciples' (Acts 9:1), but he was really persecuting Jesus (v 4).

Persecution does not only affect the church adversely. It has positive results as well. The church is purified, refined and matured as it passes through such testing. You really discover who your friends are, who are plastic in their Christianity and who are real, who love Jesus more than their own lives and comforts, who are prepared for blessings through buffetings, and who are willing to allow suffering to work for God's great glory.

A number of Christian leaders in Britain are beginning to predict that a period of persecution is coming for the church. Already the signs can be seen. If some left-wing councils have their way, civil liberties and police protection will be withdrawn from any group of people who do not affirm 'positive images of homosexual and lesbian lifestyles'. The battle is on as Christians begin to confront such policies.

In education, as parents and Christian teachers begin to voice their views against the teaching of homosexuality as a normal way of life and heterosexuality as discriminatory or even abnormal, they are discovering the cost of holding such views. Intimidation, lack of career development opportunities, even public ridicule are already being seen.

But this is only the tip of the iceberg. If persecution is to come upon the church, these are merely the opening shots in a war of attrition. Verbal sniping will sooner or later give way to much more open methods of persecution.

But spiritual warfare isn't just the passive suffering of persecution—even though that has a direct outcome in that Satan is overcome 'by the word of their testimony'. Spiritual warfare has a much more 'attacking' element about it. And prayer is the means whereby we can go on the offensive against Satan and his powers. After all, we can't see him; we can't identify the Enemy in any recognisable form. We may see the effects of his working in some of the social and moral evils in society, or in the spiritual realm through cults and the occult. We may choose to do something to correct these evil effects—we can 'wage war' on sex shops, or obscenity or crime—but we won't in the process deal with the root causes, only the symptoms.

Prayer gets at the root. The means of attacking the devil have to be spiritual, because he is a spiritual being. If we can only understand God by his Spirit (see 1 Corinthians 2:10-15), then we can only oppose Satan by the Spirit of God. 'The weapons we fight with are not the weapons of the world. On the contrary, they have divine power to demolish strongholds' (2 Cor 10:4).

In the inevitable clash with the powers of evil arrayed to overthrow the work of God, no assumed authority will avail. Going through the motions is not good enough. Words alone, no matter how religious, have no intrinsic power. Prayer is a clash of rival authorities, and the enemy will only yield to the authority that is personally related to Jesus Christ.[7]

The late Samuel Chadwick said, 'Satan dreads nothing but prayer. His one concern is to keep Christians from praying. He fears nothing from prayerless studies, prayerless work, prayerless religion. He laughs at our toil, mocks our wisdom, but trembles when we pray.'

No wonder, then, that as God creates a spirit of praying and a movement of prayer, an almost insatiable hunger for his presence among his people, Satan trembles. No wonder that in times of spiritual 'refreshing from the Lord' it seems that Satan's mouth is shut—for a while at least—and his works nullified. No wonder heavenly power breaks through the heavenly realms, and heavenly holiness falls on earthly people. No wonder that God is at work and whole communities know about it! Prayer has defeated Satan, the battle is won and God's will is being done on earth as it is in heaven.

I believe that in revival Satan is powerless in the face of the sheer volume of believing prayer from those who, trustingly looking to God, wait with faith and confidence for assured answers. He cannot counteract such prayer. Or, as with those ladies in the Hebrides, the faith of a few, who know what they are doing as they agonise in sacrificial prayer, prevails and overcomes the Evil One. At such times Christ is with us in our praying. 'As believers we are in Christ and he in us, and this means that his aggression against Satan must be expressed through us.'[8]

At the same time, Christ always lives to intercede for us (Heb 7:25). So he and we together present an invincible alliance to counteract Satan's purposes!

Notes

1.   Graham Kendrick and Chris Rolinson *All Heaven Waits* (Thankyou Music, 1986).

2. R Arthur Mathews, *Born for Battle* (STL Trust, 1978), p 34.
3. I R Govan, *Spirit of Revival* (Faith Mission, 1950), pp 204–205.
4. First published in Restoration magazine, and reprinted in *Sound of Revival* (Summer 1984).
5. *World Church Digest*, Kenya.
6. Arthur Wallis, *China Miracle* (Kingsway, 1985), p 148.
7. R Arthur Mathews, *Born for Battle* (STL Trust, 1978), p 109.
8. *ibid*, p 13.

11

Know Your Lord,
Know Your Enemy

When I was a young Christian someone told me, 'Know your Lord, know yourself, know your Enemy.' Yet in my thirty-five years as a Christian, I can only remember three or four times when I heard anybody teaching about Satan. There must be thousands, if not millions, of Christians who do not know what he is like, how he works and how to combat him and win—not only for their own self-protection, but also so that they can liberate others.

Unless we have an adequate knowledge of our Lord's triumph and glory, and our place in it, we cannot engage in spiritual warfare effectively. We will not be able to engage meaningfully in intercessory prayer, and our revival praying will lack power. We cannot prevail and overcome the 'deeds of darkness' (Rom 13:12) unless we have put them aside ourselves, woken up from our slumber and clothed ourselves with Christ.

And unless we know Satan's identity, and are familiar with his techniques and strategy, we cannot oppose him effectively in the heavenly realms. If we do not know in what ways he is vulnerable, we cannot defeat him.

If we long to see a general spiritual awakening, we must discover how to pray in the Spirit with all kinds of prayer and, 'having done all to stand', how then to go on the offensive against the gates of hell.

> In warfare there are four possible attitudes—offence, defence, detente or desertion. It is the first one of these attitudes that our enemy fears, for Satan trembles when he sees the weakest saint upon his knees. He will therefore do all in his power to put God's people on the defensive, there to talk detente or else to frighten them into deserting.[1]

Revival praying is prayer on the offensive. Therefore it is spiritual warfare. And it is Spirit-prompted, Spirit-initiated, Spirit-inspired and Spirit-sustained.

Revival has been described as 'the revelation of the Spirit of Jesus'. 'Jesus is Lord' is not just a theological statement, it is a fact, a declaration of faith; it is a denial of any other 'lords'. He is Lord over the cosmos, over creation and over the church. He is Lord over principalities and powers. They are under his feet, defeated at the cross, cowed · into submission to Christ's ultimate authority, and we share in that sense of victory, triumph and reign. So before we look at our Enemy, let's be sure we know our Lord.

Know your Lord: who we are in Christ

God did not bring us to himself just for our own personal blessing. Praise God, we are blessed with all kinds of spiritual blessings in the heavenly realms in Christ (see. Ephesians 1:3), but his purpose for us is more than that.

He doesn't leave any of us in an isolated limbo state. Part of his purpose is to bring us into *relationship*—vertically and horizontally. Just as I receive from others, and also share with others, so I receive from God and I also give back.

1. We're in the family of God the Father

That means that we have a heavenly Father who delights to give good gifts to his children—to us. So when we come to him in prayer, we do not have to wait until we are granted an audience. We can come boldly to the throne of grace. Those who are sure of their security and relationship with God sometimes seem audacious and ambitious in what they request from God. Their faith in his ability to answer is not conditioned by their own feelings or fears, but by the prospect of his greatness (see Daniel 10:15-19).

It also means that we have brothers and sisters—people with whom, and to whom, we belong. People who are also in Christ. So in prayer warfare it is vital that we express 'family' in mutual care and prayer. The Christian 'family unit' is larger than a mere nuclear family. It is made up of all races, languages, colours, ages, nations and denominations.

We need to recognise that that spiritual family identity is a source of strength in prayer. There is no room or need for isolationism in spiritual warfare. We need one another.

And we need to watch for every device that Satan employs to destroy that sense of family. We must resist him in Jesus' name.

2. We're in the church of Christ the Son

What is the church? Scripture gives us two pictures to help us.

First, it is the body of Christ through which his will, his ways and his word are communicated in our world. Secondly, it is the bride of Christ which shows the closeness of the relationship that we have with him. He values us, gave himself for us, equips us, and one day he will be reunited with us in glorious splendour at 'the wedding supper of the Lamb' (Rev 19:9).

We are members of his body. That means we draw our energy from him. The fullness of his Spirit gives us power to do his will and purity to be like him in holiness. Christ is our Head. We are all functional parts of his body. When each part is working properly, it harmoniously builds up and strengthens other parts. And we move in perfect co-ordination from the Head, to manifest him in the world.

That means we need to be linked to other members of his body. 'Go-it-alone' Christians will not triumph. They may survive, indeed they *should* survive for Christ's Spirit is within them, but they won't share in the victories that other parts of the body achieve for the glory of the Head. We're in his church, as body and bride, and we are linked to others who are also in his church, across the fences that our man-made structures have erected to keep us divided.

Satan's work is to divide the church—from each other and from the Head. So it follows that Christ's will is the opposite.

We can only survive and be victorious in spiritual warfare if we are united in Christ. He wants us presented to himself 'as a radiant church, without stain or wrinkle or any other blemish, but holy and blameless' (Eph 5:27).

3. We're in the kingdom of Christ the King

The Bible describes Christ's kingdom as an everlasting heavenly kingdom, the kingdom of God and of his dear Son. It is entered by new birth (Jn 3:3); it is a kingdom of 'righteousness, peace and joy in the Holy Spirit' (Rom 14:17). Being in the kingdom means that we serve Christ the King. His rule in our lives is paramount. What he wants done must be done out of loyalty and love.

We will obey because we love the Lord. That means

there is no room for self-will; we cannot follow inclinations that may be contrary to God's will. He reigns in us,
in others who are in the kingdom and in society, if we are
prepared to extend his kingdom into areas and situations
that are not yet part of his domain.

So today people talk of kingdom life, kingdom
principles, kingdom schools and kingdom businesses.
Because we are in his kingdom we also share in his
victory over the works of darkness, the kingdom of
Satan, and his victory over the kingdoms of this world
when they are brought under Christ's control. 'The
seventh angel sounded his trumpet, and there were
loud voices in heaven, which said: "The kingdom of the
world has become the kingdom of our Lord and of his
Christ, and he will reign for ever and ever"' (Rev
11:15).

Christ's rule is to extend over our thought processes
and values, our physical needs and desires, our attitudes
and actions. He must be Lord of our families, our
relationships, our habits and our behaviour. His lordship
needs to be mediated through every area of life which we
touch. Our purpose is to be the channels of his rule in
those areas where other gods are followed.

Where spiritual warfare is concerned, it is vital for us to
know, theologically and in our experience, that Christ is
reigning now. 'Now have come the salvation and the
power and the kingdom of our God, and the authority of
his Christ. For the accuser of our brothers . . . has been
hurled down' (Rev 12:10).

Christ has already conquered Satan and sin (see
Revelation 1:18) through his death and Resurrection. He
has 'disarmed the powers and authorities [terms used to
denote Satan's agents in the heavenly realms], he made a
public spectacle of them, triumphing over them by the
cross' (Col 2:15). 'The true order of faith is not that
we have to live an earthly life with a view to heaven,

but a heavenly life with a view to earth,' comments Dr Stuart Holden.[2] So we go into battle not from the perspective of our circumstances here on earth, but from our position above in Christ. We pray *from* victory, not *towards* it.

4. We're in the army of the victory of Calvary

We have a heavenly leader, the 'captain of our salvation'. 'Army' is not a term used in the Bible to denote any kind of relationship we have with Christ, but there is an army of the Lord: 'I saw the beast and the kings of the earth and their armies gathered to make war against the rider on the horse and his army' (Rev 19:19). Terminology is used to help us understand the nature of what we're in. The Christian life is a battle, not a picnic. We're in a war against Satan. There are victories to be won. We have armour to put on and weapons to use. And it is very important that we put on the full armour of God.

I have described that armour in detail elsewhere (in my book *Three Times Three Equals Twelve*), so I shall not deal with it here. But the fact that there is a battle is the important thing to grasp, and also that we need to be aware of Satan's strategies and tactics in our struggle so that we can stand, overcome and win!

> The bitter enmity of Satan is now directed against the Church in order to vent his spleen against the Head through the members of his body. His fiery darts zero in on those who have not learned to take their position in the heavenly places with Christ by faith and who face life without taking to themselves by prayer the whole armour of God.[3]

5. We're in the heavenly realms

Paradoxically, we are citizens of two worlds: the earthly and the heavenly. We live on earth, yet we're also seated with Christ in heavenly places. Ephesians has most to teach us about those heavenly 'realms' (NIV) or 'places' (AV). The word means literally 'heavenlies', or 'above the sky'.

We can deduce that there are different levels or strata in the heavenlies. The sky, or cosmos, can be taken as the first level—the physical, visible heavens that God created. Paul writes about 'a man' being 'caught up to the third heaven', which he deduced was paradise (2 Cor 12:2–4). He heard 'inexpressible things' there.

Paradise is only mentioned three times in the Bible: by Jesus to the dying thief and to the church in Ephesus (Rev 2:7) where the angel refers to the 'paradise of God', and by Paul in 2 Corinthians 12. So we can conclude that the third heaven is the dwelling-place of God, or at least his angels. That means there is a second level, which, it seems, is what Paul is referring to in the Ephesian letter, as the place where 'principalities and powers' dwell and operate.

He tells the Ephesians that Christ was raised from the dead by God who 'seated him at his right hand in the heavenly realms, far above all rule and authority, power and dominion, and every title that can be given, not only in the present age but also in the one to come' (Eph 1:20–21). His was a place of power and unrivalled authority, to be occupied for all time and eternity.

This is a potent verse. Paul compares the power that God employed in raising Christ from the dead and placing him at his right hand with the power that is 'for us who believe'—an incomparably great power. There is nothing like it in time, nor in all creation. It surpasses all others because it is beyond measure. And this power, that is just as great as the Resurrection, Ascension and glorification of Christ, is for us who believe. Hallelujah!

In Ephesians 2:6, Paul goes further:

> God raised us up with Christ and seated us with him in the
> heavenly realms in Christ Jesus, in order that in the coming
> ages he might show the incomparable riches of his grace
> expressed in his kindness to us in Christ Jesus.

The verbs are in the past tense, not the future. In other
words, we are *already* seated with Christ in the heavenly
realms. This is not a nice, theoretical, theological conun-
drum. It is truth for us to grasp in our spirits, not merely
with our minds.

Because I am already seated alongside Christ in the
heavenly realms, in the presence of God, I am already
there, spiritually speaking. I can begin now to realise and
enter into the victory that Christ has already won, the
power that he now has and exerts, and the character that
is his.

This understanding of our present position in Christ
has all sorts of implications for us individually, and for
us as the church of Jesus Christ on earth. If only we
could be more aware of the fact that we are *already*
citizens of heaven, and less aware of our human con-
straints on earth!

In Ephesians 3:10, Paul goes further still. God's intent
'was that now, through the church, the manifold [or
many-faceted] wisdom of God should be made known to
the rulers and authorities in the heavenly realms'.

That is neither past nor future tense. It is the present
tense. God is intending and waiting for the church—*his*
church—to enter into the conflict and make known his
marvellous varied wisdom to the chiefs and authorities in
the heavenlies.

It's a present-day ministry which the church hasn't
begun to enter into, or fathom, or fulfil to anything like
the extent which God intends. It's a ministry for the
church, not for the individual. It implies a sense of

corporate ministry, even of unity with all who are 'in Christ' anywhere. What is implied here is the sense of unity across denominational barriers, often a feature of revivals.

The 'observable unity' of Jonathan Edwards' book needs to be seen not as a passive thing, but an active expression of what and who we are in the heavenlies in Christ.

It means that we do not stay in the earthly realm, behind our fences. What is implied by Ephesians 3:10 is a church united in prayer, reaching heaven, God's holy dwelling-place.

So before we enter into spiritual conflict with the powers of darkness, we must be aware of our position in Christ and enter into the experience of it. And we must be much more conscious of who we are in Christ than what we were in the world.

Know your Enemy: Satan's methods

In any war, intelligence sources give information about the enemy—who he is, what his resources are, how they are deployed, what his plans and objectives are and so on.

The feeding back of such information becomes vital for the formulation of strategy and tactics to defeat the enemy, by thwarting his intentions and overcoming his forces. There may be many battles on the way, some of which will be lost, others won, but before we go into battle, we must know who and what we are up against.

Satan is a fallen angel. Isaiah 14:11–17 and Revelation 12:7–9 describe something of what happened as Satan was cast out of heaven for the sin of pride and false ambition. He was a chief angel. He had authority over some angels, who were cast out of heaven with him. It appears that a third of the angels was involved.

He can assume different guises – a dragon, a serpent, a lion, a scorpion – all of them depicting fearsome, vicious beings. He 'masquerades as an angel of light' (2 Cor 11:14). Sometimes the word 'devil' is more accurately translated 'the accuser of our brothers' (Rev 12:10).

Satan has principalities and powers under his domain. We also know that evil or unclean and demonic forces were at work in Jesus' day as he encountered Satan's influence in the demoniac of Mark 5, the boy who suffered from fits in Luke 9 and even the apostle Peter (Mt 16:23; Lk 22:31).

Christ had some uncompromising things to say about Satan, as he bluntly told the religious leaders of his day what he thought of them.

> You belong to your father, the devil, and you want to carry out your father's desire. He was a murderer from the beginning, not holding to the truth, for there is no truth in him. When he lies, he speaks his native language, for he is a liar and the father of lies (Jn 8:44).

So if we want to know who we're up against and what he is like, we can have no better authority than Jesus. He implies in John 10:10 that Satan is a thief who delights to 'steal and kill and destroy'. Human nature in its sinfulness mirrors his basic faults: wanting to be like God, being proud in his own conceits, seeking to gain applause, popularity and worship. The dictators of this world display the traits of corrupted power. 'Power corrupts, and absolute power corrupts absolutely.'

In his deeds, Satan always reflects his character. He tries to get us to be and to do what he is and does. He tries to suggest that we can do without God, not only intellectually, but also in everyday real–life situations. 'I did it my way,' becomes a philosophy and not just a song. He gives us delusions of grandeur, inspiring us to think more highly of ourselves than we ought. Thus the imaginations of our mind in the realm of fantasy too often get translated into reality, frequently with tragic results.

Satan's strategy further reflects his character. In his attacks upon the church and family life, and in his constant antagonism to the Godhead (see diagram), he sows seeds of discord and dispute in several ways.

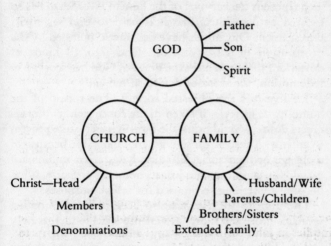

Satan's purpose is to divide every part of these and to sever connections between church, family and God.

1. Satan tries to rob us of our inheritance in Christ

He does this by challenging the truth of God's word and then contradicting it. He did it in the Garden of Eden. He did it when he tempted Jesus in the wilderness. He does it with us. By suggestion, subtlety and innuendo he casts doubt on what God has said. He will even use Scripture to suit his own purposes, so that man ends up exchanging the truth of God for a lie, and worshipping and serving creatures rather than the Creator (see Romans 1:25).

In the wilderness he set out to rob Christ of his earthly task and his heavenly relationship. If he had succeeded there would have been no cross, no Resurrection and no hope for mankind.

2. Satan seeks to raid our instincts as humans

Sex and survival are basic human urges.

Sexual desire is at its strongest in the teenage years, but its purpose is the survival of the human race. Satan has so twisted both instincts that it is hard to find sex in its purest form. Our minds have become so polluted by the prostitution of this gift from God into all kinds of deviation, that even after the grace of God has worked in redemption, the seeds of deviation remain.

We live in a sex-obsessed society. The spread of the homosexual lifestyle, if taken to the conclusion its protagonists desire, would bring the human procreative process to an end. Abuse of those who are vulnerable because of their age or their social situation has scarred millions of people for whom sex has lost its beauty. For many, it has become something to be used for selfish purposes.

The urge to survive has also been polluted. Conflict escalates more and more, as violence leads to increasingly cruel ways of displaying distorted aggression. Attitudes of murder, greed, violence or self-indulgence are all expressions of satanic influence; so too are terrorism, unrighteous trade, power struggles, abortion, soaring suicide figures and character assassinations. The Enemy has done this.

It is perhaps hardly remarkable that in times of spiritual awakening, many of these aspects of modern life decline, or even disappear.

3. Satan attempts to render us ineffective

He does this by making us absorbed either in ourselves or in our circumstances. Introversion, introspection, self-pity, depressive illnesses, self-justification—all these are evidence of self-absorption.

Satan doesn't enjoy being reminded of what he is like. (That's why people engaged in teaching, writing or the practice of spiritual warfare always seem to have a hard time!) I remember seeing an episode of *Star Trek* on television, in which the only way to destroy the prevalent evil force, who lived in a pit, was to surround it with mirrors. When it rose from the pit and saw itself in the mirrors it was so torn between its self-esteem and its hatred of itself that it exploded.

Satan is trying to do precisely that to us. He wants to make us focus on our guilt, our moral and spiritual weakness and the circumstances in which we are placed, so that he will be able to create despair and sow the seeds of self-destruction. And the end product of continuous self-absorption and despair is suicidal thoughts, and eventually suicidal acts. Something snaps. The response to self-hatred or oppressive circumstances is to push the self-destruct button.

But effective living and effective service depend on having a very different focus. They depend on us having our focus on God. When Christ is put first, the rest of life gets in balance.

In his *Dynamics of Spiritual Life*, Richard Lovelace shows that historically the church has always grappled with the reality of Satan and his influence.

If the church suffers spiritual decline and the world and the flesh prevail among its members, the enemy can recapture lost ground and imperil the very life of the Kingdom. Even when the church is on the offensive the strategies of darkness can be baffling and destructive ... The destructive malice of Satan against all humanity, and particularly against the church, is channelled through human agents and the systems and institutions they have built.[4]

The church in Korea has discovered how through prayer the power of Satan over families, over institutions, over areas and over a nation can be broken.

> As we learn to pray in the Holy Spirit, realizing that we have been given authority, we are able to bind the forces of Satan in people, communities and even in nations: However, because Satan is a liar and the father of lies, he tries to convince us that he is in control. But as we learn to fast and pray and exercise our rightful spiritual authority, Satan and his forces must yield to the will of God.[5]

It is not enough, however, to know about Satan and how he works. We must also learn how to counteract his devilish devices and how to win that heavenly realm battle which will, I believe, be the forerunner of a heaven-sent revival. And that is what my next chapter is about.

Notes

1. R Arthur Mathews, *Born for Battle* (STL Trust, 1978), p 51.
2. *ibid*, p 27.
3. *ibid*, p 12.
4. Richard Lovelace, *Dynamics of Spiritual Life* (Paternoster Press, 1979), pp 136, 140.
5. Paul Yonggi Cho, *Prayer: Key to Revival* (Word, 1984), p 35.

12

Combating Demonic Forces

We have already seen that revival praying is praying that
has the 'extraordinary' about it. And the 'extraordinary'
is that which takes time, requires effort, involves sacrifice
and is prepared, like the desperate widow in the Bible
(Lk 18:1–8), to wait until an answer is received from
God.

If it takes all-night prayer, so be it. If it takes forty
days and forty nights of fasting, as Jesus did in the
wilderness, then it must be done. If it takes the arranging
of concerted prayer on a daily basis in numerous places
throughout the country, then it must be done. It is both
the volume and the quality of prayer that is significant in
the spiritual warfare that we have to be engaged in and
win.

Prayer is a form of spiritual bombing to saturate any area
before God's army of witnesses begin their advance. Prayer
is the barrage to drive back the demon hosts which are
determined to stop the triumph of Christ. Prayer is the
invincible force to break down every opposing wall, to
open every iron gate and every fast closed door. Prayer
penetrates every curtain of darkness. Prayer crumbles every
bastion of darkness. Prayer demolishes every fortress of hell.

155

Prayer is the all-conquering, invincible weapon of the army of God.[1]

So wrote Dr Wesley Duewel.

Writing to the Ephesians, Paul says:

> For our struggle is not against flesh and blood, but against the rulers, against the authorities, against the powers of this dark world and against the spiritual forces of evil in the heavenly realms. Therefore put on the full armour of God (Eph 6:12–13).

After outlining what that armour consists of, he continues:

> And pray in the Spirit on all occasions with all kinds of prayers and requests. With this in mind, be alert and always keep on praying for all the saints. Pray also for me, that whenever I open my mouth, words may be given me so that I will fearlessly make known the mystery of the gospel (Eph 6:18–20).

Spiritual warfare means encountering the forces of darkness through prayer. Satan and his minions are so entrenched in their activity on earth and in the heavenly realms that a great deal of concerted and concentrated praying is needed to shift him and to force him to relinquish his hold.

In one sense, Christ has already gained the victory. Having 'disarmed the powers and authorities, he made a public spectacle of them, triumphing over them by the cross' (Col 2:15). In other words, the purpose of the cross was not just to bring us eternal salvation, and into a relationship with our loving heavenly Father. It was also to 'destroy him who holds the power of death—that is, the devil—and free those who all their lives were held in slavery by their fear of death' (Heb 2:14–15). John reminds us that 'the reason the Son of God appeared was to destroy the devil's work' (1 Jn 3:8).

So Christ has already won the victory over Satan, sin and death. Because he triumphed over Satan on the cross, was resurrected from the dead and ascended to the Father's right hand, he can also say, 'I am alive for ever and ever! And I hold the keys of death and Hades' (Rev 1:18).

In another sense, however, believers are to make that victory of Christ their own, by faith, in their own personal situations. In the same way, Christ's death on the cross—in order to take away our sin—was a fact in that it happened nearly 2,000 years ago, but it needs to be appropriated by those who exercise saving faith in order for it to become personal experience to them today.

We do not only enter into spiritual warfare from an earthly perspective. We are also involved on the basis of our position in Christ in the heavenly realms. We share in the victory. We need to grasp hold of that in our spirit, as well as with the theological understanding of our mind. Because we share that victory, we should be in a position to make it a reality in the situations we are concerned about.

Entering into Christ's victory, however, isn't just a theoretical matter. We need to know *now* that he is reigning over every area of our lives. There is no room for compromise, a critical spirit or defeatism.

In spiritual warfare, when we are challenging the forces of darkness, Satan will look for the weak points in our armour and in our character and then attack. We are vulnerable unless we continue to stand with our shield of faith in place to withstand the fiery darts of the Evil One. We are more vulnerable when we are on our own than when we are in prayer with others. But we can stand if we are 'strong in the strength that God supplies through his eternal Son', to quote from the hymn 'soldiers of Christ arise'.

Paul was able to take the authority that Christ had given to him and withstand Elymas the sorcerer. He was able to say to him very bluntly, 'You are a child of the devil and an enemy of everything that is right! You are full of all kinds of deceit and trickery. Will you never stop perverting the right ways of the Lord?' (Acts 13:10). And then Elymas was struck blind.

If we have ambiguity in our lives, and lack true faith in the Son of God, we shall be no better than the Jews in Ephesus—like the sons of Sceva who were set upon by an evil spirit (Acts 19:16). If we attempt to engage in spiritual warfare while tolerating wrong in our lives, we will be as compromised as they were. But if we stand complete in Christ we have every right to withstand the Evil One, to resist the devil, to proclaim Christ's victory over him, and by faith to start spoiling his goods, after we have first learned how to bind him.

In prayer, when we are praying against the works of Satan, we can begin to proclaim and affirm our belief and trust in all that Christ has accomplished. Satan cannot stand people lifting up the name of Jesus. Just as in Christ's day demons had to cower in the presence of deity, so today Satan's agents will be forced back when Christians take their stand as God's agents on earth, since Christ's Spirit is living and active within them.

But how do we engage in spiritual warfare, and what should our strategy be?

We need to be clear about our immediate objectives

It is no good going into spiritual warfare with all guns blazing in every direction. We need to decide not only *who* we are up against, but *what* we are up against.

In each situation, we should ask: Are we battling

against principalities in the heavenly realms? Have we discerned what those principalities are? Or are we on this occasion praying against satanic influence in a particular individual?

Answering those questions involves identifying our immediate objective. Here are a few of the options open to us:

1. Prayer may be a means of engaging in *a holding operation*, to hold ground and prevent demonic forces from doing further damage. This is often the case when we and others are praying for an individual. When there isn't sufficient time to deal with the issues; when there is inadequate information; when we haven't discerned specifically what we are up against, it may be all we can do: simply to commit the person prayerfully to the protection of the Lord, while we in prayer seek to discover what to do next.

2. We may have as our immediate objective *the taking of prisoners*. In other words, we may desire to bring people under the domain of our Commander-in-Chief. That's what I would call 'evangelistic' praying. We want to see people brought out of darkness into God's marvellous light, translated from death to life, released from the power of Satan into the liberty of Christ.

When we pray like that, we are praying against Satan's influence in people's lives. It may call for spiritual discernment to identify obstacles that would prevent them from exercising faith and from receiving the Holy Spirit.

3. We may want to *recapture lost territory* or an Enemy stronghold. Some places are so full of the presence of evil you can sense it. It's even so in some churches. In the letters to the Churches in Revelation, the influence of Satan is recognised. The Church of Smyrna had those who were 'a synagogue of Satan'. The Church of Pergamum dwelt 'where Satan had his throne . . . where

Satan lives'. The Church of Thyatira had some who had 'learned Satan's so-called deep secrets', under the influence of Jezebel. In each place the Christians had to overcome all that was wrong, and hold on to what they had.

So if we are attempting to recapture such a territory or stronghold, we need discernment to know when we should engage in such a battle.

We should go to prayer at a time when we can cause the Enemy maximum damage. For example, yours may be an area where witchcraft is prevalent. Or perhaps a famous spiritualist is having an evening seance at your local town hall. The Enemy may have gained entry to a school or college, and consequently Christianity and its influence has been nullified. Concentrated prayer for those establishments can change things!

Find out when the witch's ceremonies are to be held, when the seance is advertised to take place, what the teaching hours are at the school. Gather your praying forces during those times, and pray confusion into the ranks of the Enemy.

4. Fourthly, you may want to *liberate an area*. You are looking at a housing estate or high-rise flat and in the name of Jesus you long to see Christians in-filtrating that area and making a bridgehead by plant-ing a church. Before they can do so the area needs to be liberated, and that is a task of spiritual warfare in prayer.

The Church of England has an old ceremony known as 'beating the bounds', when Christians would walk round the parish rather as if proclaiming territorial rights. In similar fashion, prayer warriors can walk round an estate or a building in order to free such locations from the influence of Satan and to prepare them for the sowing of the word of God. Such prayer is part of the softening-up process.

Richard Harbour, now a minister in Manchester, used to live in the area where I now live. He tells me that in those days they hardly knew a Christian on the estate, but that he and his wife used to walk up and down the streets praying, asking the Lord to work in the area. Today, even though it is many years since Richard and his wife lived in my neighbourhood, there are Christians in almost every street, and we have a thriving church that was planted in the area in 1982. I am sure that it was the prayers of Richard and Shirley Harbour, and many others who have moved into the area since, that prepared the ground.

5. You may want to *win a skirmish*. It may be a Bill before Parliament, or a proposal for a local sex shop, or a crucial meeting of the local council. All may contain elements of satanic influence where you long to see a spiritual breakthrough for the glory of God. Prayer is the key to the overturning of policies and practices that are contrary both to the will of God and to the good of the community.

6. We may be the *support troops* for somebody else's assault on Enemy ground. An evangelistic mission may be being planned. The degree of success will be directly related to the amount of believing prayer, not only for the individuals who are to hear the gospel, but also against the powers of darkness that will hinder its proclamation and its effect. There are so many examples of evangelistic missions either failing because of little or no prayer, or succeeding because of the presence of much prayer.

7. Last, but by no means least, our immediate objective may be to *change the whole spiritual climate in our nation*. This is the big one! If that is our aim, we must prayerfully discern the main ways by which Satan has exerted his influence historically and in contemporary society. What principalities do we discern are subtly, surreptitiously but surely at work?

Revival praying is relevant here. Do we want to see an outpouring of God's Spirit on our nation? Then we must, at some stage in our praying for such an awakening, come strongly against the prevailing powers of darkness.

It isn't something we can enter into automatically. We may have to wait on the Lord until we see that it is the right time to engage in such an encounter, and we need to wait, too, for God to give us appropriate information regarding the particular situation we are facing.

We need, then, to be equipped with a clear understanding of our immediate objectives. But we also need, as warriors in the spiritual battle, to know what weapons we have available.

We need to understand the resources that we have available in our spiritual warfare

1. First, there is *prayer in the Spirit*. Paul talks about praying with his spirit as well as with his mind (1 Cor 14:15). In context, he is referring to praying in tongues, for he who speaks in a tongue 'utters mysteries with his spirit', or, 'by the Spirit' (v 2). Prayer with the spirit also includes the groans and the intercession that the Spirit makes on our behalf and through us (see Romans 8:26–27). The Holy Spirit who lives within the child of God is involved in the praying that goes on. When we are directed by the Spirit in spiritual warfare, he sometimes interprets to us the specific things we should concentrate on and what God's desire is in the matter.

This does not mean that we are thus isolated from the Father. On the contrary, prayer in the Spirit is very much in tune with the will of God. It is the work of God.

2. We also have available *the sword of the Spirit* in prayer: the Bible, the spoken word of God or the 'now' word from God given by the Spirit. When he was tempted by the devil in the wilderness, Jesus used Scripture each time to counteract Satan's taunts. The Old Testament prophets likewise recorded their prophecies by saying 'thus says the Lord'.

3. As Paul reminds us (Eph 6:18), we battle with *all prayer*, with all kinds of prayers and requests. That includes supplication, petition, thanksgiving, praise, intercession, listening to God, asking, seeking and knocking.

4. The *name of Jesus* is given us as a 'weapon' in our praying. Jesus invites us to bring him our requests, when he says: 'I will do whatever you ask in my name, so that the Son may bring glory to the Father. You may ask me for anything in my name, and I will do it' (Jn 14:13–14). Jesus repeats that promise in John 15:7,16 and in John 16:23–24. He surely means us to get the message that using his name in prayer is not just adding a phrase that guarantees anything we may care to ask for, but that through using the name of Jesus we are indicating that our requests are in line with his will and purpose too.

In bringing healing to the man at the gate of the temple, Peter and John acknowledged its source: 'By faith in the name of Jesus, this man whom you see and know was made strong. It is Jesus' name and the faith that comes through him that has given this complete healing to him, as you can all see' (Acts 3:16).

5. We have available to us *the blood of the Lamb* and *the word of our testimony*. In the picture recorded for us in Revelation 12, the accuser is overcome by the blood of the Lamb and the word of the testimony of the brothers who are accused. It is they who 'did not love their lives so much as to shrink from death' (Rev 12:11). The blood of

Jesus Christ, God's Son, cleanses us and keeps cleansing us from all sin. Symbolically the blood on the doorpost and the lintels, when the children of Israel came out of Egypt, was their safeguard against the influence of the angel of death. The fact that Jesus as the Lamb of God has taken away our sin means that we have the protection of his shed blood. We do not use the blood to fling at Satan, but we can say, 'Demonic powers have no rights here.' We are claiming the protection that the shedding of Christ's blood gives us. 'If the Son sets you free, you will be free indeed' (Jn 8:36).

6. Finally, we can use *aggressive elements* in our fight against the demonic forces. In the story of Jehoshaphat going into battle in 2 Chronicles 20, we have a picture of a man who trusted in God.

First of all he proclaimed a fast for all Judah. When they came together they sought help from the Lord and he led them in a model prayer, where they affirmed their trust in the living God by saying, 'We do not know what to do, but our eyes are upon you' (v 12). As the people waited in the presence of God—wives, children, little ones—God spoke through his prophet Jahaziel. And as he spoke, he gave the strategy that God intended them to use in order to overcome the vast army that had come against them.

In response to this word of prophecy, early the next morning Jehoshaphat went with the people and appointed musicians and singers to lead the army into battle. It was as they began to sing and praise the Lord that God set ambushes against the men of Ammon and Moab and they were defeated. I believe that once we have prayed and sought God and heard his word to us, we can then praise him, and as we do so we shall see him confuse the Enemy.

Also, God may sometimes give us a strategy which

includes chanting or shouting the word of God and even the blowing of trumpets as occurred in the capture of the city of Jericho. Because God is God, he sometimes leads us to do the unusual in our spiritual warfare. Our responsibility is not to ask questions, but to obey.

We can use our prayer warriors as we would an army, by deploying them in what the Roman soldiers used to call a 'phalanx' in order to do battle. I have been in a prayer gathering where it seemed right to ask everybody to stand, then turn outwards away from the inner circle as if we were marching out into battle, and then pray simultaneously for a city or for an area.

Groups, too, can be strategically deployed. Christians in Birmingham had a united open-air prayer gathering. Small groups were then sent to the various institutions and important civic locations to pray.

We might want to take a small company of people, as Gideon did when he surrounded the enemy's army. He had split his tiny army into three groups of 100 each. Theirs basically was a trumpet-blowing operation. God did the rest. 'The weapons of our warfare are not carnal, but mighty through God to the pulling down of strongholds' (2 Cor 10:4, AV).

Binding and loosing

I want to add a word about 'binding and loosing'. This is a complex area and the Bible does not speak very clearly about it.

The idea appears three times in the New Testament. In Matthew 12:28–29 Jesus says:

If I drive out demons by the Spirit of God, then the kingdom of God has come upon you. Or again, how can anyone enter a strong man's house and carry off his possessions unless he first ties up the strong man? Then he can rob his house.

In Matthew 16:18–19, Jesus is talking about the ministry he has given to Peter when he says: 'On this rock I will build my church, and the gates of Hades will not overcome it. I will give you the keys of the kingdom of heaven; whatever you bind on earth will be bound in heaven.'

The same verse is repeated in Matthew 18:18. There is a variation of these verses in Mark 3:26–27: 'If Satan opposes himself and is divided, he cannot stand; his end has come. In fact, no-one can enter a strong man's house and carry off his possessions unless he first ties up the strong man.'

The strong man is equated here with Satan. We are told that what is done in relation to the binding of satanic powers on earth will be as if they are bound in heaven. The 'binding' has to do with the imprisoning aspect of Satan's agents in order that his goods can be spoiled. The 'loosing' has to do with the releasing from captivity of those who have been 'all their lifetime subject to bondage'.

In any spiritual warfare we need to be aware of spiritual leading in the here-and-now. We cannot enter into the battle merely relying on yesterday's victories or strategies. We need fresh instructions for every battle. It is a spiritual war, not a natural one.

Someone has written:

If the people of God only knew and laid hold of the weapons God has given them, they would arise with a shout of victory! Instead of being depressed and talking about the blackness of the outlook in the world, the powers of darkness that have come down upon the whole Church of Christ could be shaken off. There are physical and nervous breakdowns, divisions injuring God's work, extraordinary tangles in missionary affairs, so great that some of God's saints do not know where to turn. Here is the key, take the victory of Calvary and bind the strong man by prayer so that he cannot hinder God's work.[2]

'Who will storm hell's stronghold?' asks Leonard Ravenhill. 'Who will deny himself good food or good company or good rest, that hell may gaze upon him wrestling, embarrassing demons, liberating captives, depopulating hell and leaving, in answer to his travail, a stream of blood-washed souls?'[3]

Prevailing prayer breaks through the cosmic conflict of principalities and powers. When we engage in spiritual warfare, we can begin to break Satan's power by conquering in the heavenly realms those principalities and powers. Each engagement will be different. Therefore, we need to listen to the voice of the Spirit, to learn from him what he is seeing and sensing about particular needs, particular timing, particular emphases and particular tactics. In our praying we will be in accordance with the will of God and yet sense his anguish in fulfilling it.

The whole of heaven is waiting for the church to take its place in the spiritual battle. The whole of heaven's host is standing ready to act on God's behalf. God is waiting for people to stand in the gap, to pray prayers of repentance and confession as we take upon ourselves the heartbreaking needs of mankind. He is also waiting for us to come strongly and aggressively against the powers of darkness, knowing that as we do so we have all the resources of the Godhead available to us. When we pray such strong prayers, Satan's power is challenged and he is made to relinquish his hold, his influence is nullified, he is forced back. He has to surrender—not to us as God's agents on earth alone, but to the risen Son of the living God in whose name we come against him.

However, a word of warning. Both Peter and Jude warn us in their epistles about the danger of going too far. Peter warns us about people who despise authority: 'Bold and arrogant, these men are not afraid to slander celestial beings; yet even angels, although they are stronger and more powerful, do not bring slanderous accusations against such beings in the presence of the Lord' (2 Pet 2:10–11).

Jude tells us that 'even the archangel Michael, when he was disputing with the devil about the body of Moses, did not dare to bring a slanderous accusation against him, but said, "The Lord rebuke you!"' (Jude 9). It is much better in spiritual warfare for us to ask the Lord to rebuke Satan and to bind him. That way we know it will be done, because Satan has to bow to Christ.

He is not yet under our feet. But he is under Christ's feet.

Notes

1. Wesley Duewal, quoted in *Kneeling We Triumph* (Harta–Flame Publications, 1971), p 44.
2. E F & L Harvey, *Kneeling We Triumph*, Book 2 (M.O.V.E. Press) p 49.
3. Leonard Ravenhill, *Why Revival Tarries* (STL Trust, 1972), p 41.

13
Highway Through The Heavenlies

'Do you believe in angels?'

It's a question I sometimes ask at prayer seminars. Most people say 'yes', though very few have owned up to having met one. But I've heard stories of people who have been visited by angels, and I've read a book in which a certain pastor claimed to have had regular angelic encounters.

None of the accounts is, of course, verifiable. You have to accept them by faith. But then the same is true of the various appearances of the risen Christ following his Resurrection. No Bible-believing Christian would hesitate to affirm them as fact. We do so by faith, and Christ's Resurrection in bodily form is crucial to our faith.

And yet our view of angels and our view of the Resurrection are often radically different. We may not doubt what happened in Christ's time, or at other times if the events are recorded in the Bible, but we may well view present-day stories of angelic appearances with some suspicion or even scepticism.

Are we denying, by our attitude, that God is able to send angels any more? Or are we merely reflecting human reluctance to believe unsubstantiated stories or supernatural happenings?

I once learned of a man, not a Christian, who was painting the outside of his house. He was interrupted by the sudden appearance in mid-air of a visitor dressed in white. He hurried down from the ladder, fell on his knees and confessed his sin to God. Then he ran to see his local vicar, who took him to a friend of mine who shared the gospel with him for the first time. Was it an hallucination, or had something really happened? We shall never know—and it doesn't really matter, since whatever it was, it brought the man to the point of seeking God.

What are angels?

Angelic visits have been a phenomenon throughout biblical history. The Bible describes angels as heavenly messengers sent to do God's bidding, or as warriors, recorded in Revelation and Daniel 10. They are also 'ministering spirits sent to serve those who will inherit salvation' (Heb 1:14). God 'makes his angels winds, his servants flames of fire' (Heb 1:7; cf Ps 104:4). An angel appears after the Fall as a guardian of the way to the tree of life (Gen 3:24). Angels also appear in the last book of the Bible—in fact the whole book is an angelic revelation of the future as given to John on the Greek Island of Patmos. The book is authored from heaven!

God's angels are usually despatched on important heavenly business. Their role and function is seen in what they do.

They give protection

They protect God's holy character by thwarting the purposes of Satan and of man in his unregenerate sinful state. They give protection to God's people in the face of human adversity and danger. 'He will command his angels concerning you to guard you in all your ways; they will lift you up in their hands, so that you will not strike your foot against a stone' (Ps 91:11–12). 'The angel of the Lord encamps around those who fear him, and he delivers them' (Ps 34:7).

They respond to our prayers

As Daniel prayed and fasted for twenty-one days, two angels of God fought and overcame the demonic Prince of Persia. They breached the heavenly realms to bring God's answer to Daniel's prayer (see Daniel 10:1–14).

Angels went into battle too in response to Elisha's prayers, when the Arameans surrounded the city of Dothan. Elisha knew the angels were there—the hills were full of horses and chariots of fire. He prayed that his servant might see them, and then asked God to use them to inflict blindness on his enemies (cf 2 Kings 6:15–19).

God's angels go into action not just at his command, but also in response to the specific prayers of God's children. In the Acts of the Apostles, when the church prayed for Peter in prison, it was an angel who brought him to freedom unnoticed (Acts 12:5–10).

They speak God's word

Almost all the Old Testament patriarchs had personal encounters with angels who had come to bring God's message to them. The prophets, such as Ezekiel, Daniel and Zechariah, testified to the word of God coming to them by way of heavenly visitors. And an angel visited Mary and Joseph to bring God's announcement of the birth of Jesus.

They mete out God's judgements

In Hezekiah's day, one angel slew 185,000 men in the Assyrian army. When the time came for Moses to lead the children of Israel out of Egypt, the angel of death went through the land and slew the firstborn in every home. The Book of Revelation is a book about angels. From chapter 8 onwards they are involved in a terrifying and awesome sequence of events in which the final confrontation and eventual destruction of Satan's purposes is depicted. They were sent to rescue Lot and his family from Sodom, but they were also sent to destroy it (Gen 19:13).

They rejoice at God's victories

'There is rejoicing in the presence of the angels of God over one sinner who repents' (Lk 15:10). They rejoiced at the birth of Jesus, and I expect there was great rejoicing when he returned again to his Father after the Resurrection. Myriads of angels joined their voices together to sing: 'Worthy is the Lamb, who was slain, to receive power and wealth and wisdom and strength and honour and glory and praise!' (Rev 5:12).

Angelic visitations

In his remarkable book *Angels: God's Secret Agents*, Billy Graham describes many instances of extraordinary appearances of angels in our contemporary world—some culled from other authors, some personal stories told to him. He writes:

> Reports continually flow to my attention from many places around the world telling of visitors of the angelic order appearing, ministering, fellowshipping and disappearing. They warn of God's impending judgement; they spell out the

tenderness of his love; they meet a desperate need; then they are gone. Of one thing we can be sure; angels never draw attention to themselves but ascribe glory to God and press his message upon the hearers as a delivering and sustaining word of the highest order.[1]

And I have read at least one testimony that speaks of frequent appearances of angelic beings—often in the middle of the night.

I don't need to be persuaded and convinced about the present-day ministry of angels. They are for real! Most of us don't see them, but they are around us and constantly minister to us, fight for us, protect us and guide us. But some people, I believe, do have a heightened spiritual sensitivity, and it is good to have their stories of angelic appearances.

Elisha saw angels; his servant didn't. Saul of Tarsus saw a brilliant light as he met Jesus on the road to Damascus; those with him didn't see it, but they heard the sound. Was it the intensity of that 'light from heaven' which flashed around him that caused his temporary blindness? Peter, James and John saw Jesus transfigured (literally, metamorphosed) before them. 'His face shone like the sun, and his clothes became as white as the light' (Mt 17:2).

Many of the biblical accounts of angelic appearances record this same intensity of light. It seems that anything or anyone that came out of heaven shone with the glory of God, with sparkling brilliance and indescribable beauty. Moses, coming out of the presence of God, shone so much that his fellow Israelites could not bear to look at him; they had to cover their faces. The people of God will one day 'look and be radiant' (Is 60:5) after the revelation of God's glory comes upon them. So much so that 'nations will come to your light, and kings to the brightness of your dawn' (Is 60:3).

Angelic roles in revival

Why all this talk of angels in a book on 'preparing for revival'? The reason is that I believe any consideration of the ways in which God works in times of spiritual visitations must take into account *all* the biblical options. And the ministry and visitation of angels is so common in Scripture that we must expect them to be involved in something so extraordinary as a spiritual awakening.

Most historical accounts of revival do not include stories of angelic visitations. But that doesn't mean that their presence was not revealed, nor that they were not involved. On the contrary; angels are invisibly involved all the time in the outworking of God's purposes, but because so many incredible things happen in divine visitations, we must be open to the possibility of angelic *appearances* in any future revival.

We are familiar with the unseen awareness of God's presence. We know that when he breaks through the heavenly realms in power and in strength—when he visits a person, a place or a nation—the sense of his presence is awe-inspiring. We know about the convicting, powerful work of the Holy Spirit in people's lives, which takes place in the context of scenes that are usually extraordinary to people.

But though the Spirit's work is unseen, the evidences of his power are often uniquely visible. What causes the physical, tangible awareness of the presence of God? What brings people from their homes in the middle of the night, as if drawn by some mighty magnet, to seek God?

Could it not be the presence of angels in strength?

Historical revivals

Most historical accounts of revival are carefully documented. The late Dr J Edwin Orr, whom we have already mentioned as the world's most prominent historian of spiritual awakenings, would not include anything in his many volumes on revival unless the information he received, read or researched could be substantiated. But the trouble with angelic appearances is that they usually *can't* be substantiated. Angels don't seem to want to wait around for us to call our friends, contact the television studio, or summon the local press! Consequently we have to be content with hearsay. We have to trust the integrity of the witness.

Angels in modern revivals

In today's stories of God's working, there are many accounts of angelic sightings. Frequently they appear to non-Christians, who perceive that solitary Christian workers are surrounded by men or an army, or protected by people dressed in white. John G Paton, a missionary to the New Hebrides, described how one night a hostile crowd of tribesmen intended to burn down his home and kill him and his family. He and his wife prayed all night and at daybreak the local warriors inexplicably left. A year later the local chief was converted. When asked about the attack a year earlier, the chief said, 'Who were those big men you had with you? There were hundreds of them dressed in white with drawn swords surrounding the mission station.' The natives were afraid to attack.[2]

During the cultural revolution in China, extraordinary things happened as the church in China was not only preserved but grew phenomenally. In some areas over half the population became Christians. In some cities one-eighth of the population belonged to house churches. Some communes changed in six months from being almost entirely communist to being almost entirely Christian. Elderly pastors or Christians became the leaders of this new-born, rapidly-expanding church. Leslie Lyall, a statesman in relation to Christian work in China, is reported to have said that in the rural areas as many as 90% of the population are Christians.

In the midst of this remarkable movement of God's Spirit, there were many indications of angelic interventions. Happily many of these have been written down. I am indebted to the research of the late Arthur Wallis for the examples that follow.

In 1975 there was a church that used to hold retreats and training classes for young converts. They were having a baptismal service for one hundred converts when militia men arrived to prevent the baptisms. However they saw soldiers surrounding the Christians, and so withdrew their detachment.[3]

The 'soldiers' were from the heavenly army. They enabled the baptismal service to continue without interference.

A pastor was about to be executed because he refused to stop preaching the gospel. He was allowed a last request before being shot.

He replied that he would like to sing a song. Since it was a public execution, permission was granted. He sang out in a booming voice the praise of God, and as he sang the sky began to light up with the splendour of God's glory, and all the people that were gathered round heard what sounded like thousands of voices singing along with the pastor. Shaken by the incident, the authorities decided to postpone the execution while an urgent telegram was sent for advice. The telegram found its way up the bureaucratic ladder until it reached the Premier Chou en Lai ... he replied, 'This is no ordinary man. Release him and don't even bother him again.'[4]

Arthur Wallis also gives many examples of supernatural healing, that is, where the instrument of the healing has been angelic, and where there has been corresponding urgent and earnest, although not necessarily prolonged, prayer.

Both Scripture and history seem to suggest that as God's people pray and the power of God then breaks through in a given area, an opening is created in the heavenly realm. This enables the angels to mediate God's will, character, presence and power on an extensive scale. Suddenly the powers of darkness are forced back. They have to relinquish their hold in the face of such power from God, which is linked with the power of prayer.

We have seen that Scripture has many examples of angelic visitations in answer to prayer. An angel visited Cornelius in answer to his prayer (cf Acts 10:2–4). When the children of Israel cried to the Lord, he sent an angel to Gideon to commission him to lead his chosen people into victory over the Midianites (Judg 6). It was when Daniel prayed that an angel was immediately despatched with the answer from God's throne (Daniel 9:20–23).

It's recorded, however, that a second time it took three weeks for the angel to overcome the Prince of Persia and reach earth with the answer. In other words there was a battle going on in the heavenly realms—the battle in which the child of God or church of God on earth is involved.

It is a spiritual battle, fought with spiritual means and spiritual forces—a battle that has *already* been won in the context of eternity. Christ has already conquered Satan, sin and death. He has disarmed principalities and powers, triumphing over them in and by the cross. Satan is and has been overcome 'by the blood of the Lamb and by the word of their testimony' (Rev 12:11). Jesus has put away sin by the sacrifice of himself. He is alive for evermore.

And yet, that victory which was achieved through the cross, burial and Resurrection of Christ 2,000 years ago, as far as heaven is concerned, has still to be mediated to every nation and every generation, and appropriated by faith by the family of God on earth. God needs us, his agents on earth, to co-operate with his angels from heaven in extending that victory. It is a victory that may take time and effort to be experienced—the effort of sacrificial prayer.

A highway through the heavenlies

I find it helpful to think pictorially about this, and the picture I have is of a highway through the heavenly realms being opened up. When that highway is constructed, it provides a broad channel for the release of supernatural power on a vast scale. With the increasing volume of prayer from the church in many countries has come an increasing release of spiritual power.

Today the church in many countries of the world is experiencing a prayer movement. In 1984 there was the first International Prayer Assembly in Korea (see Appendix). David Bryant of the Lausanne Committee for World Evangelization has the marvellous task of encouraging Concerts of Prayer worldwide. National leaders are finding out from each other how to call the church in any nation to pray for its own nation and the nations of the world. The church in Korea is in prayer twenty-four hours a day, 365 days a year for the growth of the church worldwide. The Evangelical Alliance Worldwide Week of Prayer (held each year during the first week of January) involves 1,000,000 Christians in Europe alone.

That highway through the heavenlies is conceptualised by Isaiah. Chapter 35 talks of the highway being 'the Way of Holiness' (v 8). Those who walk in it are followers of 'the Way'—the redeemed and the ransomed of the Lord. If we link Isaiah 57:14 and 62:10 together, we see that the highway has to be built up. The way has to be prepared, obstacles have to be moved out of the way, stones need to be removed. Preparing the way for the King of kings was not just something the disciples had to do so that Jesus could enter Jerusalem triumphantly. We today have to remove all obstacles so that the glory of God can be revealed.

God wants that highway opened up. Now is the time to prepare it.

But *how* can that happen? It seems to me that the volume of prayer, or the earnestness and extraordinary nature associated with the praying, builds up a climate of increased spiritual activity in the heavenly realms. As God's people pray, the powers of darkness are forced back. Their power begins to be taken away, their purposes begin to be frustrated. Because Daniel continued praying and partially fasting for three weeks, the angels of God were able to penetrate that 'second level' occupied by Satan's angels.

What would have happened if Daniel had stopped praying earlier? Would the angels have broken through? Probably not. While the believer is in prayer he is providing a bridgehead, a foundation on which the rest of the superstructure of spiritual victories can be built. Daniel had 'set [his] mind to gain understanding and to humble [himself]' before God (Dan 10:12). The spiritual intensity of his encounter took his breath and speech away. 'I am overcome with anguish'—that was *after* his prayer was answered (v 16). The nature of Daniel's prayer had been to 'mourn'—literally to bewail, to lament.

There are thousands of prayers that are never answered because God's people do not persist in believing prayer, and because they do not recognise the nature of the spiritual battle in the heavenly realms. God is in his holy dwelling. He has myriads of angels at his disposal, but he does not force his will on us. When, however, our desires are in line with his will and are expressed in believing prayer, the angels are released into action. Daniel had two despatched to him. 'The chariots of God are tens of thousands and thousands of thousands' (Ps 68:17). They need a highway through the heavenlies.

A ministry for the church

That highway is established when God's people are at prayer. Although we are citizens on earth, when we pray we are occupying our position in the heavenly realms where we *are* seated already with Christ (Eph 2:6–7). As we—the church—begin to pray, we are in effect fulfilling God's purpose that 'through the church, the manifold wisdom of God should be made known to the rulers and authorities in the heavenly realms' (Eph 3:10).

That is a present-day ministry for the church. It is entered into on the basis of unity between Gentile and Jewish believers (see Ephesians 2:18; 3:6). Therefore it requires unity among Christians within those camps as well as across them. God's people being together in purpose, love and trust are then able to approach God in faith and in freedom, with complete confidence in his ability to hear and in his power to answer. His answer, Paul says, is capable of being 'immeasurably more than all we ask or imagine' (Eph 3:20).

Do we want to build up a highway for the King? Do we want God's enemies to be scattered? Do we want

to see a release of God's power on a scale that is
breathtaking and awe-inspiring, bringing the glory
of God and the powerful presence of God into our
world—and our nation? If we do, we must pray. We
must make that highway through the heavenlies.
We must clear the rubble of demonic blockage and
boulders out of the way; then his angels will 'pass
through'.

We must create, in the desert around us, 'a highway
for our God'. There must be a massive preparation in
which 'every mountain and hill [is] made low; the rough
ground shall become level, the rugged places a plain'
(Is 40:3–5).

When a motorway is constructed, a great deal of time
is spent making cuttings through mountains, building
bridges or viaducts over valleys. Rubble has to be shifted,
rocks have to be hewn out. The process of levelling the
road is long, arduous and time-consuming. But in the
end, traffic flows freely in both directions. God is waiting
for that highway through the heavenlies similarly to be
made.

When God's people are sufficiently in earnest to
clear, by prayer and action, some of the obstacles
to the extension of Christ's kingdom, then we shall
see a spiritual breakthrough. The first to go must be
obstacles in the church: obstacles of pride and self-
centredness; obstacles of lukewarmness and lethargy;
obstacles of criticism and cynicism; obstacles of pet
doctrines and petty differences. Then, obstacles in
the society around us, which by our silence we have
tolerated. There must be genuine repentance for the
sins of the nation. We must 'stand in the gap' on
behalf of the people. We must plead on their behalf
before God. We must, like Jesus, bear the sins of
many and intercede—that is, we must stand in their
place.

The picture I draw from Scripture is that as we create that highway in the heavenly realms by prayer; as we are in earnest and in faith for God to confound and confuse the powers of darkness; as we add to that a highway of holiness in the spiritual desert around us; then God will break through in power, glory, majesty and might. 'The glory of the Lord will be revealed, and all 'mankind together will see it. For the mouth of the Lord has spoken' (Is 40:5). We shall be called 'the holy people'. We are that, but we shall also become it. We shall be a revelation of brilliant radiant light—not a glimmer, not pin-pricks of light, but an effusion of incandescent power.

I have a vision of an army of angels with the chariots of God, passing through the heavenly realms and visiting us to bring the glory of the Lord to earth.

It won't catch us, God's people on earth, by surprise—we've been praying for it. But it will cause us to be filled with awe and wonder and delight. That army of angels will not come to just one congregation or denomination, but to the praying people from all congregations and denominations. And then they will go out into the spiritual wilderness around; into those areas to which we have already been by prayer and action; into the prisons, into Parliament, into the inner cities, into broken homes, into schools and colleges—even onto radio and television. For 'all flesh shall see it together'.

I am talking about a spiritual awakening, not the Second Coming of Christ—though the former will be a kind of practice run for the latter. And my prayer is that he will not come in judgement as he did for Sodom and Gomorrah, but that he will give us time to usher in his kingdom and prepare the spiritual highway.

Notes

1. Billy Graham, *Angels: God's Secret Agents* (Doubleday, 1975), pp 24–25.
2. *ibid*, p 3.
3. Arthur Wallis, *China Miracle*, (Kingsway, 1985), p 176.
4. *ibid*, p 175.

Section III
Who Wants Revival?

14
Who Wants Revival?

In preparing to write this book, I've read a great many books and articles on revival. I've heard many sermons on the subject, given both by people who have experienced revival and by people who long to do so but can only speak from other people's experience. I have talked to many eye-witnesses, and I have attended conferences. I have spoken about revival and published occasional articles. But, so far, my only experience of revival has been at the personal level. I have not yet seen it in the sense I've been exploring in this book: corporate revival, the kind of revival in which a whole community is affected.

Which leaves me—and many of you who are reading, because you are in the same position—with a question to answer. *How do we change things so that we can begin to experience what others have experienced?*

In this last section of the book, I want to draw on the views of many historical and contemporary Christians. What do they see as the will of God for his church, and what do we have to do to become ready to experience an outpouring of God's Spirit?

British Christians of my generation, it must be said, have been very good at being spectators. We were brought up on church services led by a single (male) person, and if we were handed the right things to say or sing we sometimes joined in. From our segregated rows we looked past the backs of other people's heads to the performance that the preacher or leader of the service was giving. We didn't know very much about 'audience participation'.

Today we are seeing a healthy change for the better, with the introduction of more freedom and participation in worship and prayer. Yet, even so, many of us hold on to a spectator mentality. We are glad enough to be 'blessed', informed, or even challenged, but we don't often get involved in the action. And younger men and women of a new breed seem to be setting the pace, rolling up their spiritual sleeves and getting involved in costly ministries.

That takes commitment, concentration and power. Many of us are content to stand on the sidelines and watch, but do we really want to be standing there when revival comes, contenting ourselves with applauding and cheering when we hear about God at work in somebody else's church or area?

We can't simply wait for the day of God's power to come to our doorstep and then switch to being participators. The coming of that day requires that we be participators *now*, by prayer and waiting on God. In the Old Testament we find that Azariah the prophet told King Asa, 'If you seek [the Lord], he will be found by you, but if you forsake him, he will forsake you.' And we are told that King Asa and the people 'entered into a covenant to seek the Lord, the God of their fathers, with all their heart and soul' (2 Chron 15:2,12). Similarly, the amount of earnest praying we do is undoubtedly an indication of how much we really want God to be at work in our nation.

I was once having a meal with Tom Houston, formerly Executive Director of the Bible Society and now International Director of the Lausanne Movement. He issued me with a challenge: 'Brian, what would you like to have achieved by the end of the 1980s?'

I thought about it for a moment and then replied, 'I'd love to have seen a spiritual awakening; to be able to say, "I was there."'

I wasn't merely wanting to be a spectator, and I wasn't just wanting to be the objective reporter who passes on the story to people who weren't there—though I must confess that there is something exciting about a scoop! What I really meant was that I wanted to share the experience of the apostle John, when he said: 'That ... which we have heard, which we have seen with our eyes, which we have looked at and our hands have touched—this we proclaim' (1 Jn 1:1). He wasn't just one of the spectators. He was close at hand; he was sharing in the most intimate moments of his Lord's life, involved behind the scenes, being a part of the purpose for which Christ had come and continuing with it after he had gone.

I want to see revival. It's a great longing of mine; one with which I would love to inspire you. Years before my lunch with Tom Houston, I woke in the middle of one night with tears in my eyes, crying out to God to send a spiritual awakening to Britain. That might seem like emotionalism. I believe it was much more than that. The Holy Spirit doesn't disappear when we turn the light off at night. I believe God was building up in me a desire which I would not have had so strongly otherwise. And I also believe the Holy Spirit is the divine communicator—sharing the feelings and burdens from God with us.

To some, it might seem as if God was playing melodramatic games with me. But the whole experience of

God's people and God's word denies that. Many who live close to God have the same desire and the same burden. They have dreams, visions, hunches, emphases in their sermons, a deepening sense that something is about to happen. You can read about such things in the Bible and in Christian biographies. You can see them in the lives of Christians today. The Scriptures are full of such stories. God does entrust some people with his secrets.

He is still the same God. And I believe that he is telling many people today that revival is on its way!

So, who has he been speaking to, and what has he been saying?

People of history

In a private letter written in the late 1970s, the late J Edwin Orr both rebuked me and challenged me to look more closely at history. So I began to do so, and soon I realised what he meant.

There is no doubt that the people whom God has used in revival have very often been the people who hungered and thirsted for revival. They have sought him, they have prayed fervently and at length, they have been honest and realistic in repentance and heart-searching, they have wanted nothing to stand in the way of God carrying out his work and his will through them.

Take William Chalmers Burns, for example, who came to Kilsyth in Scotland in 1839 to hold special meetings. He took his sermon illustrations from the great revival at Kirk of Shotts two centuries earlier. 'He felt his own soul so moved that he began to plead for instant response,' Orr wrote in his letter:

All the while the people were rapt in solemn attention. Then their feelings broke and weeping and prayer drowned out the voice of the speaker. Some were screaming out in agony; others—among them strong men—fell to the ground as if they had been dead. The revival swept Kilsyth, and all the denominations worked together in perfect harmony. Then the awakening spread all over Scotland.

Evan Roberts was an ardent student of the history of revival from his boyhood. He wrote to a friend: 'For ten or eleven years I prayed for a revival. I could sit up all night to read or talk about revivals. It was the Spirit that moved me.' He wrote to his brother, Dan, before the Welsh revival began, telling him that great blessing was coming. To his brother-in-law, Sidney Evans, he said: 'I have a vision of all Wales being lifted up to heaven. We are going to see the mightiest revival that Wales has ever known. Do you believe that God can give us a hundred thousand souls now?'[1]

God chose Roberts in 1904 as his instrument to bring revival to Wales—a revival that had repercussions throughout the world. A hundred thousand souls were indeed saved. It took six months.

Orr himself had a similar experience. In 1951 he visited many parts of South America, speaking about revival and illustrating his message by reference to the great revivals of the past. Eighty churches in Sao Paulo, Brazil, responded. They began to pray each week for revival. In 1952 God answered by sending revival throughout Brazil, and Orr was one of God's chosen instruments of revival.

In eighteenth-century England, George Whitefield was God's instrument to spark revival and, in 1740, to fan the glowing embers of the Great Awakening which had begun under Jonathan Edwards in 1734 in New England. Whitefield was a man who spent whole days prostrate before God in earnest prayer. Like his contemporaries, the Wesleys, he was a man 'whose heart was after God'.

A warning note was sounded by Thomas Charles, the architect of the Calvinistic Methodist tradition. He wrote, 'Unless we are favoured with frequent revivals, and a strong powerful work of the Spirit of God, we shall in a great degree degenerate and have only "a name to live".' That doesn't mean, of course, that future revivals have to model themselves on past ones, and it doesn't mean that revival is going to solve all our problems. Indeed, each revival has brought fresh problems, as Jonathan Edwards, writing about contemporary revival, acknowledged: all revivals are 'mixed' works of the Spirit. They have their excesses. But they are nevertheless works of God.

W E Sangster pointed out that 'passionate, pleading, persistent prayer is always the prelude to revival'. When that sort of prayer is absent it is an indication of the value, or lack of value, many Christians place on it. Some see revival as something extraordinary (which it is) and therefore an optional extra. Because they do not see the desperate need for revival, many never bother to ask God for it.

Duncan Campbell's hunger for revival was sharpened by what he had himself seen God do in the Hebrides. He told the Keswick Convention:

It is one thing to shout it, it is one thing to sing it, it is one thing to talk about revival, but give me a people on their faces, seeking to be rightly related with God, and when that happens, we will soon know the impact of God-realization in our country. We do not pray for revival in order that souls may be saved, but souls are saved in their thousands when we have revival; when the thirsty are satisfied, then the floods come on the dry ground.

How is it that we see so little of the supernatural in operation? If Christianity is a religion, not of aspiration alone, but pre-eminently of fulfilment, how is it that revival tarries?

Is there any reason why the Church today cannot every-where equal the Church at Pentecost? We are afraid of disturbing people today. You must not have their emotions stirred, you must not have people weeping in a meeting, you must not have people rolling on the floor under con-viction of sin (or jumping as they did in Wales in the mid 18th century, or being prostrated by the Spirit, as occurs frequently in times of revival). Keep things orderly, we say. May God help us, may God have mercy upon us. Who are we to dictate to Almighty God as to how he is going to work? If God chooses to move in that way, if God chooses so to convict men and women of their sin that they will be about to lose their reason, I say, God move on until we see again what was witnessed in the revivals of Edwards' day, Finney's time, in the 1859 revival, in the Welsh and Hebridean revival—God moving in super-natural reality.[2]

Do we want a revival in our day? Do we really, sincerely, longingly want to see God at work in our land? James Burns, writing in 1909 in *Revival, their laws and leaders*, said:

To the church, a revival means humiliation, a bitter knowledge of unworthiness and an open humiliating con-fession of sin on the part of her ministers and people. It is not the easy and glorious thing many think it to be, who imagine it filled the pews and reinstated the church in power and authority. It comes to scorch before it heals; it comes to condemn ministers and people for their unfaith-ful witness, for their selfish living, for their neglect of the Cross, and to call them to daily renunciation, to an evangelical poverty and to a deep and daily consecration. That is why revival has ever been unpopular with large numbers within the church. Because it says nothing to them such as they have learned to love, or of ease, or of success; it accuses them of sin, it tells them they are dead; it calls them awake, to renounce the world and follow Christ.[3]

People of today

I believe that God is making people hungry today for an outpouring of his Spirit. Many prominent Christian leaders sense that we are on the verge of something awesome and wonderful. I know, too, that he is leading many people to make a commitment to pray sacrificially—by getting up early every morning for prayer, and by seriously fasting.

Dr Orr has said:

> There is neither theological nor historical nor sociological reason to forbid the hope of another great ingathering. Whether the English-speaking world will first experience another religious Awakening or another baptism of fire of a crueller kind is a matter of conjecture.[4]

Many are cautiously wondering whether in fact when God does move supernaturally again in Western Europe, it will be associated with a time of persecution. And if we do face such a time, will the opposition come from militant politicians on the extreme left as they pursue policies which are anti-God and anti-Christ, and which discriminate against Christians? Or will it come from those who are clearly under the domination of Satan, followers of witchcraft, Satanism, spiritism and other forms of occultism as they kick back against the church's opposition to their devilish practices and influence? Will it come from commercial interests, as they see their profits falling, as concerned Christians rise in opposition to their exploitation of the vulnerability of others? Or will it come from the expanding influence of the Muslim world, which is pouring millions of pounds into Britain in a concentrated effort to convert it into an Islamic state by the end of the century?

It is certainly true that in other times and places, persecution has sometimes been a prelude or a consequence of revival.

It is a point taken up by Paul Yonggi Cho in his book *Prayer: Key to Revival*: 'We are at a crucial point in the history of the church. The enemy knows that the hour is late and is poised to attack every Christian family, church and organization.[5]

That attack may come in the form of outside opposition and violence. Or it may come from within, as Satan tries to divide families (especially Christian families) or to sow the seeds of bitter divisions in the church, so making us ineffective and powerless. Cho goes on:

> At no time in the history of the modern world has there been such an outpouring of Satanic influence as there is today. The bottom of the pit of hell is belching out its filth in murder, rape, pornography, lawlessness and so on. Just as the preaching of the Wesleys kept Britain from following France in revolution in the eighteenth century, so too a new outbreak of revival can bring about the social and political changes necessary to keep us from international destruction and calamity.[6]

> If you desire revival, there has never been, nor are there now, any short cuts to revival. The only key to revival is prayer. However, it must begin in you and me.[7]

But how does one prepare for revival? And will we recognise it when it comes? Will God pick up one or two key people as he has done before, and use them like comets, blazing into the universe with a trail of light behind them?

I find that some believe that when God does move this time, he won't use famous people, though no doubt future historians will identify one or two extraordinary characters. I myself believe that God will move through the community of the church, spreading through the land by means of his body which is awakened, watchful and full of expectancy. I have been praying that he would work through children and unknown young people.

Then, when the world sees God working through the young—many of whom are casualties of twentieth-century life—no glory will come to man. When God uses the unknowns, we will have to say, in awe and wonder, 'The Lord has done this, and it is marvellous in our eyes' (Ps 118:23).

Notes

1. J Edwin Orr, *The Flaming Tongue* (Moody Press, 1973), pp 4, 6.
2. Duncan Campbell, *The Price and Power of Revival* (Faith Mission), pp 26–42.
3. Winkey Pratney, *Revivals* (Whittaker House, 1983), p 22.
4. J Edwin Orr, *The Second Evangelical Awakening* (Marshall Pickering, 1949), p 267.
5. Paul Yonggi Cho, *Prayer: Key to Revival* (Word, 1984), p 157.
6. *ibid*, p 9.
7. *ibid*, p 158.

15
Preparing for Revival

So far we have looked generally at the history and features of revivals. Maybe your appetite, like mine, has been whetted, and you are asking, 'Can it happen here? Will it happen here? What must we do to prepare for it to happen here?'

Preparing for revival has been compared to sailing. A yacht that waits until the wind is blowing strongly before having its sails hoisted will lose ground or founder. A yacht that fails to have its sails up at all will find itself tossed about by every wave and gust of wind and will go nowhere. But a yacht that raises its sails at the first slight breeze will be ready to go with the wind. So it is with the church.

Colin Whittaker recalls a conversation he had with Paul Yonggi Cho in 1981 about preparing for revival:

Preparation for revival [Cho said] is like building a dam ahead of the rain. Even though we really desire a downpour to quench the drought, if we don't build a dam, we shall not keep that rain. If God showers down revival and individual ministers and churches are not ready to accept it, then all the blessings of the revival will be wasted. Therefore I say it is the hour for Great Britain to train the ministers and lay Christians to be ready to accept this revival.[1]

Nick Cuthbert, one of the Christian leaders in Birmingham where there has been a number of open-air prayer marches and gatherings attended by thousands in recent months, wrote to me in 1987 in similar vein. 'My main concern is that the church is prepared for revival in terms of its structures and preparedness to grow.'

A few years ago I visited the village of Baldhu, near Truro in Cornwall. I had read of the awakening that took place in the early 1850s in that area under the ministry of William Haslam, a contemporary of Billy Bray—who was once known as 'God's madcap'.

Haslam had built the parish church at Baldhu, which became the centre of the movement of God in that area. It was tin-mining country, and thousands of people were converted. It was a revival with extraordinary happenings. One meeting lasted eight days non-stop, although Haslam came and went. The Spirit was in control.

When I visited Baldhu, the church was boarded up; gravestones surrounded the church, stretching far into the undergrowth—a reminder of what the past had been like. Billy Bray's memorial stood at the entrance to the church. A mile up the road was one of his chapels. I sat in the chair he sat in, stood at the pulpit from which he used to preach, and cried at the top of my voice, 'Lord, do it again—in my day.'

We shall do nothing in preparation for revival unless first of all we *desire* it. And that desire is not a desire of the flesh, like a lust; nor a desire that is temporary or fluctuating, like a passing fad or the latest Christian interest. It is a desire that is expressed in a willingness to do whatever God asks of you, whatever that might mean, however inconvenient it might appear, and no matter what the cost in sacrifice of time, effort, interests or money.

Stephen Olford has written:

If there is to be a revival of spiritual life and power, it must originate with the individual believer...The sin, which is spoiling the life of the Christian, must be judged and put away. The selfishness, which is robbing Christ of the love and devotion which are his due, must be confessed and removed. The ambitions and desires, which are hindering the work of God, must be uprooted and thrown on the refuse heap. A renewal of blessing is dependent upon the restoration of communion and the reconsecration of heart and life.[2]

I have quoted many sources in this book—mainly because some of what I have wanted to say has been said or experienced by others before. At this point, however, I am asking God to examine my own heart and prepare me for revival, because all that revivalists say is necessary, is necessary for me too. As we read what others who have lived close to God and have experienced what he has done in revival, have to say, will you join me in asking God to turn our survey of his sovereign workings into something personal for yourself?

Lord, bend me

Before a nation, community or church can be affected by revival, God wants to revive each of us as individuals. We can't pray, 'Revive us Lord,' until we individually are ready to pray, 'Lord, revive me.'

Evan Roberts' oft-repeated prayer in the Welsh revival—and one that was taken up by the cries of others—was, 'Lord, bend us. Lord, bend me.' Although the reviving of an individual may actually take place at the same time as many other individuals (and usually does) there needs to be a readiness for God's reviving work to be personal.

Dr A W Tozer, a twentieth-century prophet who knew God and spent much time in his presence, gives us the following ten pointers to personal revival.

1. *Get thoroughly dissatisfied with yourself.* Complacency is the deadly enemy of spiritual progress. The contented soul is the stagnant soul. When speaking of earthly goods, Paul could say, 'I have learned to be content whatever the circumstances' (Phil 4:11), but when referring to his spiritual life, he testified, 'I press on towards the goal' (Phil 3:12,14).

2. *Set your face like a flint toward a sweeping transformation of your life.* Timid experiments are tagged for failure before they start. We must throw our whole soul into our desire for God.

3. *Put yourself in the way of the blessing.* To desire revival and at the same time to neglect prayer and devotion is to wish one way and walk another.

4. *Do a thorough job of repenting.* Do not hurry to get it over with. Hasty repentance means a shallow spiritual experience and lack of certainty in the whole life. Let godly sorrow do her healing work. Until we allow the consciousness of sin to wound us we will never develop a fear of evil. It is our wretched habit of tolerating sin that keeps us in our half-dead condition.

5. *Make restitution wherever possible.* If you owe a debt, pay it, or at least have a frank understanding with your creditor about your intention to pay, so that your honesty will be above question. If you have quarrelled with anyone, go as far as you can in an effort to achieve reconciliation. As fully as possible, make the crooked things straight.

6. *Bring your life into accord with the Sermon on the Mount and such other New Testament Scriptures as are designed to instruct us in the way of righteousness.* An honest man with an open Bible and a pad and pen is sure to find out what is wrong with him very quickly! I recommend that self-examination be made on our knees, rising to obey God's commandments as they are revealed to us from the Word. There is nothing romantic or colourful about this plain way of dealing with ourselves, but it gets the work done. Isaac's workmen did not look heroic figures as they dug in the valley, but they got the wells open, and that was what they had set out to do.

7. *Be serious-minded.* The devil's ideas, moral standards and mental attitudes are being accepted by you without your knowing it. And you wonder why you can make little or no

progress in your Christian life. Your interior climate is not favourable to the growth of spiritual graces. There must be a radical change in your habits or there will not be any permanent improvement in your interior life.

8. *Deliberately narrow your interests.* The Christian life requires that we be specialists. Too many projects use up time and energy without bringing us nearer to God. If you will narrow your interests, God will enlarge your heart. Christ is the essence of all wisdom, beauty and virtue. To know him in growing intimacy is to increase in appreciation of all things good and beautiful. The mansions of the heart will become larger when their doors are thrown open to Christ and closed against the world and sin. Try it.

9. *Begin to witness.* Find something to do for God and your fellow-men. Refuse to rust out. Make yourself available to your church and do anything you are asked to do. Do not insist upon a place of leadership. Learn to obey. Take the low place until such time as God sees fit to set you in a higher one. Back your new intentions with your money and your gifts, such as they are.

10. *Have faith in God.* Begin to expect. Look up toward the throne where your Advocate sits at the right hand of God. All heaven is on your side. God will not disappoint you.

Tozer concludes: 'If you follow these suggestions you will most surely experience revival in your own heart. And who can tell how far it may spread? God knows how desperately the church needs a spiritual resurrection. And it can only come through the revived individual.'[3]

To some, this may seem very man-centred. But man responds to what God is saying in his word, or by his Spirit. He responds to what he knows is God's will. That is obedience, and obedience is the pathway of blessing.

God will not send a spiritual awakening irrespective of what state his church is in, or what notice we take of his word to us. It matters. If he starts to convict us of things that are wrong, it is not because he is going to leave us in condemnation and guilt, but because he is going to set us

free: free to change things; free to do his will; free to
rediscover harmony and unbroken fellowship in union
with him and his people.

I heard Canon Harry Sutton say once: 'We can help
forward or retard revival—although it begins with God
as the initiator.' God is the originator of every spiritual
blessing in revival. But he doesn't do it all on his
own. He waits to work through us and with us, so that
we are partners in the outworking of his supernatural
plans. He neither wants us as uninvolved spectators,
nor as disinterested robots. What he says to us, he
says in love. And it is his love that waits for us to
respond in glad and glorious obedience—not in grudging
subservience.

However, our response may prove to be more permanent and tangible to ourselves and to others if it is
shared with another person. Norman Grubb, a colleague
of C T Studd, the English cricketer-turned-missionary,
said that revival starts

> by one person who sees from God what it is to walk in the
> light. But to walk in the light with Jesus like this involves also
> walking in the light with one another horizontally as well as
> vertically, and that means at least one other person with
> whom to walk in open fellowship. In other words revival
> starts with two people being revived, and starts at home!
> Revival is really just obeying the Holy Ghost. Where he tells
> us to 'break' (with former sins and habits) and to testify to the
> light shining on sin in our lives, and on the blood which
> cleanses from all sin, then let us obey, and we will find at once
> that the Spirit is loosed in revival in our hearts, and is moving
> in revival in the company.[4]

Sir Norman Grubb was writing from the experience of
himself and others in the East African revival, which is
still bearing fruit in the quality of lives lived through the
fires of persecution suffered by the church during the
Amin period, and afterwards, in Uganda.

Seek him

A classic example of the Holy Spirit's outpouring in which the response of man was clearly seen, is that which took place among the Moravians in the early part of the eighteenth century.

As a result of what God did at the village of Herrnhut in 1727, the Moravians enjoyed a century of continuous revival. They had a continuous twenty-four-hour chain of prayer for 100 years. And the Moravians were the sending source for a worldwide missionary movement fifty years before the first ambassadors of what we now refer to as the 'modern missionary movement' went out.

In the twenty-five years following the outpouring at Herrnhut, 100 missionaries were sent out. The historian of *Protestant Missions* wrote, 'This small church in twenty years called into being more missions than the whole Evangelical church has done in two centuries.'[5] They carried the gospel to nearly every country of Europe and to 'many pagan races' in North and South America, Asia, Africa, the West Indies and even to Greenland. Like the early church centuries beforehand, which carried the gospel to Syria, Asia Minor, Greece and the Aegean islands, the coast of Africa and into Italy within thirty years after the death of Christ, this church did the same following its Pentecost.

But it wasn't merely the personal response of already revived Christians that was significant. It was what happened at Herrnhut as the prelude to this remarkable and unprecedented explosion of Christian service that holds the key.

The first part of the year 1727 did not seem very promising. Differences of opinion and heated controversy on doctrinal questions threatened to disrupt the congregation. The majority were members of the Ancient Moravian church of the Brethren. But other believers had also been attracted to

Herrnhut. Questions of predestination, holiness, the meaning and mode of baptism seemed likely to divide the believers into a number of small and belligerent sects. Then the more earnest and spiritual souls among them began to cry mightily unto the Lord for deliverance.[6]

Count von Zinzendorf was one of their number. As their leader, he attempted to unite the followers of Huss, Luther, Calvin, Zwingli and others, by personally visiting every individual adult resident in Herrnhut. On May 12th, 1727, they entered into a covenant together 'to dedicate their lives to the service of the Lord Jesus'. The covenant was later to become the basis for linking together individual members and congregations.

A period of extraordinary prayer followed, which both preceded and followed the outpouring. It started in early July of that year, but already, for the best part of two years, there had been prayer and praise gatherings in the homes of the people. In July, they started to meet together more frequently. They poured out their hearts to the Lord, praying as they never had before. Some spent whole nights in prayer. They prayed fervently for God to pour out his blessing on the young people.

At about noon on Sunday August 10th, 1727, the preacher at the morning service felt himself overwhelmed by a wonderful and irresistible power of the Lord. He sank down in the dust before God, and the whole congregation joined him 'in an ecstasy of feeling'. They continued until midnight engaged in prayer, singing, weeping and supplication.

On Wednesday August 13th the church came together for a specially called communion service. They were all dissatisfied with themselves. 'They had quit judging each other because they had become convinced, each one, of

his lack of worth in the sight of God and each felt himself
at this communion to be in view of the Saviour.'

They left that communion at noon, hardly knowing
whether they belonged to earth or had already gone to
heaven. It was a day of outpouring of the Holy Spirit.
'We saw the hand of God and were all baptized with his
Spirit ... The Holy Ghost came upon us and in those
days great signs and wonders took place in our midst.'
Scarcely a day passed from then on when they did not
witness God's almighty workings among them. A great
hunger for God's word took hold of them. They started
meeting three times daily—at 5 am, 7.30 am, and 9 pm.
Self-love and self-will and all disobedience disappeared,
as everyone sought to let the Holy Spirit have full
control.

Two weeks later, they entered into the twenty-four-
hour prayer covenant which was to become such a
feature of their life for over 100 years. Even children
covenanted to meet together to pray, and arranged their
own special meetings. On two occasions that month
boys and girls met separately and prayed from 10 pm to
1 am. They spent the hours in praying, singing and
weeping before God. 'The spirit of prayer and supplication at that time poured out upon the children was so
powerful and efficacious that it is impossible to give an
adequate description of it.'

Supernatural knowledge and power was given to
them. Previously timid people became flaming evangelists.

Eight years later, the two Wesleys and George
Whitefield came into touch with, and under the influence
of, the power of God bestowed through the Moravians.
They gathered together with sixty Moravians and clergy-
men of the Church of England to pray at a Moravian
church in Fetter Lane in London. There, John Wesley
records, shortly after his 'Aldergate experience' of
conversion,

About three in the morning, as we were continuing instant in prayer, the power of God came mightily upon us, insomuch that many cried for exceeding joy, and many fell to the ground. As soon as we were recovered a little from that awe and amazement at the presence of his majesty, we broke out with one voice—'We praise Thee, O God; we acknowledge Thee to be the Lord.'[7]

The question is, would the work of God through the Moravians and the Wesleys and Whitefield and others ever have happened had not that small congregation at Herrnhut been real, sincere, honest, obedient and open with each other, as they sought God in earnest prayer before he visited them powerfully by his Spirit? I do not think so.

Was their response man-induced? Man doesn't naturally have inclinations towards God that involve the surrender of his pride and the confession of his wrongdoing. Surely God—even through the human leaders of the church there—had led them to consider their ways? And doesn't God always use the pleas and preaching of some, the writings of others, and the burdened praying of those who are prepared to seek God sacrificially?

As we have already seen, it is the phenomenon of extraordinary prayer which is the key to preparation for revival. The late A T Pierson has said:

From the day of Pentecost, there has been not one great spiritual awakening in any land which has not begun in a union of prayer, though only among two or three; no such outward, upward movement has continued after such prayer meetings have declined.[8]

Heal our nation

God's word to Solomon still holds true. When his people in any nation in any generation humble themselves, seek his face, turn from their wicked ways and pray, God promises that then he will 'hear from heaven and will forgive their sin and will heal their land' (2 Chron 7:14).

I do not believe the people of God have any right to expect a radical change in their land until they are prepared to come before God as the representatives of the church and the people. Not until we renew our covenant of love and grace; not until we turn from all our compromises and unholy alliances; not until we sincerely repent of our own personal sins, and the sins of the nation, can we expect God to fulfil his promise to heal our land—any land.

Repentance isn't merely a matter of repeating prayers of confession concerning the specific sins of which we are guilty as a nation (or individually). Repentance comes when we begin to feel the hurt and pain of God as he sees a nation and his people being wayward. It comes when, as we pray, God begins to communicate his feelings to us. It comes when we have learned to weep before him. It comes when, like a woman in travail during childbirth, he brings to birth in us his burden and compassion. It comes when we can cry like Daniel to God: 'We have sinned, we have been wicked, we have rebelled, we have turned away, we have not listened, we are covered with shame, we have not obeyed, we have not sought the favour of the Lord, we have done wrong' (see Daniel 9:4–11).

During 1986 in the United Kingdom there was a series of 'Pray for the Nation' evenings in over sixty towns and cities. Since then there have been days of prayer for the nation when Christians in hundreds of locations have come together to pray. The music ministry group 'Heartbeat', led by Ray Goudie, arranged Heal our Nation evenings throughout 1987 in dozens of towns and cities, appealing particularly to the younger generation with the same call to pray and intercede for our land. There have been large 'Pray for Revival' days drawing up to 11,000 people together at one venue to seek God and pray. Prayer walks and marches have brought tens of thousands of Christians into the streets to pray.

But praying for our nation and asking God to heal our land needs to continue until he visits us in mighty power. A battle is never won with one skirmish. A war needs to be fought against the powers of darkness prevalent over the land—and that requires continuous prayer. Let 'Heal our nation' be the cry of the church. But, first of all, have we sought God—for his sake?

Prayer is not an easy way of getting what we want. It is the only way of becoming what God wants us to be. Spiritual awakenings in history have always been linked to, or produced out of, a climate of prayer; not casual or occasional prayer, but sacrificial and persistent intercession.

Some while ago, while I was in prayer, I sensed that God was saying something to me which he wanted saying to his church as well. I reproduce those words here.

'Seek the Lord, you people. Seek the Lord with all your heart. Put seeking him above all other pastimes and desires. Let the hunger of being in his presence characterise your life. For when you seek him and his holiness; for when you seek him and his love; for when you seek him and his will for this nation, he will be able to come with power and purity.

'You are right to be concerned about the welfare of the nation, but above all you must be concerned for my glory, that glory might dwell in the land,' says the Lord.

'Be concerned and pray and seek my face. I am waiting to pour out my blessing, but I am also waiting for my people to long for that more than their necessary food and sleep. Seek me, my people, for unless I bless you, I will come with purging and persecution. I wish to pour out my Spirit, but I will not, and cannot, until my people take their place at my feet, at my footstool, at my throne. Come, my children, come to me in confession and repentance. Come to me to plead your nation's cause. Come to me to pray and seek my face.'

Notes

1. Colin Whittaker, *Great Revivals* (Marshall Pickering, 1984), p 179.
2. Stephen F Olford, 'Lord Open the Heavens' in *Interest* magazine (April 1981).
3. *ibid*.
4. Norman Grubb, *Continuous Revival* (Christian Literature Crusade, 1952), pp 46–47.
5. John Greenfield, *Power from on High* (Moravian Missions, 1928), p 15.
6. *ibid*, pp 19–35.
7. *ibid*.
8. *ibid*, p 66.

16
A Vision for Revival

Sing a new song to the Lord! Sing it everywhere around the world! Sing out his praises! Bless his name. Each day tell someone that he saves. Publish his glorious acts throughout the earth. Tell everyone about the amazing things he does. For the Lord is great beyond description, and greatly to be praised (Ps 96:1–4, TLB).

God's love and power, his holiness and presence, his truth and justice. These are not heavy things to make us solemn and mournful. They are not impositions to make us sterile and uninteresting. They are not doctrinal niceties to debate endlessly. They are glorious truths to enjoy, delight over and proclaim.

Whenever the people of God grasp hold of these truths with their whole beings and not merely with their minds, emotion swells up and spills over. There is shouting, rejoicing, dancing and singing. God puts the new song into our mouths. His word becomes more precious than our daily food. We delight to be in his presence. We want to sing his praise. We want to tell everyone that he loves them and can do marvels.

It is that spirit of exuberant praise and faith-sharing which the church needs to recover and which revival seems to produce. Renewal has brought about a climate of joy, but so far we are mostly keeping it within the confines of congregational meetings. When will it break out into the community?

It is when such a desire becomes almost insatiable and inexpressible, and gives birth to prolonged crying out to God, that we will see the seeds of revival planted.

Some of us are too serious about the trappings of Christianity: its observances, festivals, ceremonies and services. We want to wrap God up in a shroud of legalistic conformity, or in the cling-film of sterile ordinariness. We want to box him into our preconceived and limited perspectives, all neatly packaged, labelled and priced.

But God is not confinable. He is constantly full of surprises. He always wants to break out of our seeming normality. The variety associated with his knowledge and purposes is far too extensive for any one person, congregation, denomination, stream, language or nation to contain.

Others of us are too casual about what we believe. We know it all, but rarely let it get through to us to produce that radical change that will give us the experience of being perpetually revived. Our mind, reason and will rationalise God's word out of our experience, so that the 'obedience of faith' is not allowed to disturb our comfortable preconceived notions of Christian lifestyle.

My prayer, as we approach the end of this exploration of God's will for his church, is for us to be *abandoned to God, obedient to Christ and open to the Spirit.* That sense of abandonment says, in effect, 'Lord, you are more important than anything and anyone. Lord, I'm submitting my career, my family, my past and my future to you. I want to hold nothing back. I surrender my preconceived notions about the way you should work. I surrender my fears of letting you get too close. Lord, draw me as close as possible to you. I surrender my habits, my attitudes, my relationships, my hobbies, my timekeeping, my bank balance. It's all yours. I want to be wholly yours, devoted to you and your word, given to you and your service. Lord, show me what you want of me, and lead me into the knowledge of you and your will in every area of my life.'

Abandonment to God should include a willingness to do whatever God asks of us. Obedience at any cost is part of our abandonment to God.

At a prayer meeting of ministers recently, we sensed that God was asking us to confess to one another the sin of pride. Pride in our hearts; pride in the way we looked at our Christian ministry; pride in frequent glorying in the fruits and successes of that ministry, instead of giving God the glory; pride in our achievements; pride in our gifts.

As we prayed we suddenly realised that not only ourselves, but the church locally and nationally was riddled with pride. So what started as confession of personal pride developed into confession on behalf of the church of its sin of pride.

Normally our human pride does not allow us to confess its presence. Obedience to the voice of the Spirit was necessary in order for us to do so. It is that kind of whole-hearted and unrestrained obedience that God needs if he is to get his way with us. Without it, revival will not happen.

Such obedience will also involve openness to the Holy Spirit, an openness that will not be restricted by fear, hesitancy, or reasoned resistance. It will involve an openness and a desire for him to do anything he wants, with whoever he wishes, and whenever and wherever he wishes; and an openness to being used by him in that process. If I have such openness, it will mean that the channel of my life will be kept as unblocked as is possible, so that he can flow unhindered through me to others.

The Korean experience

It was that sense of abandonment, obedience and open- ness to the Spirit which surely set things in motion for the outpouring of God's Spirit in recent years in Korea. Just after the end of the Korean war between the North and the South in the early 1950s, God began to move. They had been enjoying seasons of refreshing since the begin- ning of the century, but now events were taking place on a new scale.

Rene Monod in his book *The Korean Revival* describes how, shortly after the war, he was invited as a missionary to speak briefly at a 5 am prayer meeting at a Presbyterian church in the capital, Seoul.

> My alarm went at 4 am. Rain was beating against my window. My first thought was, 'The prayer meeting will be cancelled because of the rain.' 'You must at least keep your word and put in an appearance, even if there's no one there but the minister,' I told myself.
>
> So at last I got dressed, rather reluctantly, and set off. The Presbyterian church came into view—a very plain building with unglazed windows. Snow and rain blew into the church through the gaping frames. I braced myself against the wind and entered the church. My eyes nearly popped out of my head—the whole place was crammed with people. There were no seats; the congregation was squatting or kneeling on straw mats. I was staggered. 'What does this mean?' I asked.
>
> 'This is our regular prayer meeting,' was the answer.
>
> 'What, in the middle of the week?' I asked incredulously.
>
> 'We come together daily,' they explained to me.
>
> 'How many people are there present?' I enquired.
>
> 'Almost 3,000—the whole congregation.'
>
> I felt dazed, and asked no more questions. Then they all prayed, all 3,000 members at once. I could feel the harmony

of the Holy Spirit in this prayer. The people prayed for nearly an hour ...

Then one of the elders asked me to give my address, adding, 'A short one, please, not longer than an hour. These people have to go to work at 7 am.' In what country of the Western world could the minister preach for an hour at a prayer meeting? What had I to say to the brethren and sisters present? It was they who had preached a sermon to me before I ever opened my mouth. In a spiritual situation of this kind I seemed to myself unutterably insignificant, tiny and pitiable.

I had not yet recovered from the shock of that first prayer meeting before I found myself attending the next one. I was drawn into the wake of this throng of praying people. For the first time I really understood the word of Acts 2:46, 'Every day they continued to meet together in the temple courts.' Every day. We pray for an awakening and nothing happens— do we wonder at it?

At the third prayer meeting of the morning I asked the brethren, 'How often in the week does your group come together to pray?' They replied, 'Every day.'

Three separate prayer groups meeting every morning! 'How long has this custom been in force?' I asked. 'Five years,' was the reply. I began doing the sums—$365 \times 5 \times 3$ comes to 5,474 hours of prayer, each attended by 3,000 people. Should we not expect such prayer to reach the throne of God?

There was a prayer service at night. Every evening a group of 100 Christians met to pray. The groups alternated, with different groups coming each evening and staying through the night—and every night for five years a hundred members of this congregation had been in prayer until dawn. Once a week from Saturday to Sunday, a thousand Christians prayed all night long.[1]

Many churches in Korea have similar practices. Most have an early morning prayer meeting—it is estimated that there are over 1,000,000 Christians in prayer in Korea at 5 am every morning. There are over 5,000 churches in Seoul alone, the largest of which has over

500,000 members. In some churches once a week the whole church is encouraged to spend the night in prayer. They have prayer mountains—and many thousands of people will be found there constantly in prayer on retreats. They reproduce diet sheets to enable people to pray and fast for days on end without damaging their health. For 365 days a year, and for twenty-four hours a day and night, there are thousands of Korean Christians in prayer. In 1980 there was a large evangelistic campaign in Seoul. The average attendance each evening was 2,000,000 people, and over 1,000,000 stayed all night to pray—sometimes in the pouring rain. Nearly half the population of Korea are now regarded as committed Christians. There has to be a connection between that and the fact that for over thirty years there has been continuous prayer occurring in Korea.

Have you a vision for revival? Do you want to see God pour out his Spirit in your lifetime and in your nation? Do you have any intuition that this is what God also wants? Have you asked him? Has he given you a quickened sense of anticipation?

If he has, then that anticipation should lead you to pray and seek God's will until the expectation is fulfilled.

God has given a vision for revival to many people. Some have kept it to themselves. Some have invested regular prayer in it. Some have multiplied it by speaking or writing of it.

Let me share with you what some are saying or have written: 'God's plan in these last days is revival in his world-wide church and through the revived church the reaping of a final great harvest of souls.'[2]

We are living in extraordinary days. The rains of revival are on the way. The cloud is already much bigger than a man's hand. All over the world there is a resurgence of living

Christianity. The coming in of the kingdom of God in our generation is a real possibility.[3]

There is no doubt that the outpouring of the Spirit is the greatest factor in the extension of the Kingdom of God.

What then are we to look for in the revival of tomorrow? Of course we want to see the people of God set on fire. We want to know that overwhelming sense of God's presence which brings the fear of the Lord. We are expecting too that powerful impact on the secular community, resulting in multitudes converted, baptized and filled with the Holy Spirit. We are looking for signs and wonders, miracles and healings performed in the name of Jesus.

But we are also expecting that many will begin to share God's heart in relation to his church. I believe that in the coming revival God will not only anoint and thrust forth evangelists, shepherds and teachers, but also apostles and prophets . . . It will be a time of sorting out for many of God's servants who are frustrated in their ministry because they have not found their true role . . . It will be a time of shaking as the Spirit of God brings adjustment to dislocated members of the body.'[4]

I have a dream that in every street in Britain there will be a cell of people who love and care for each other and reach out in loving concern for those around them. These will be the means of sharing the love of God with the immediate neighbourhood.

I have a dream that God will once again have a dwelling place among men, through whose corporate life he can reveal his glory to the world.

I have a dream that God in his abundant mercy will withhold his hand of final judgement on this nation and respond to the tears of his people and come down in a great visitation among us. In this he will reach out his hand of love to millions of spiritually starving people, adding to his church in such numbers that we are in no doubt that God has been among us, working great acts of power.[5]

I have met many people who have a vision for revival that has been communicated to them by the Spirit of God in the form of an actual vision, a dream or a picture. There is a remarkable similarity in their experiences. Some have had a vision of God moving nationally, others in their locality, but in all cases the revelation has to do with light. Light breaking through the overcast, dark sky; lights coming on in houses and streets; light flowing out like a river from a church or a town; light flowing from the North of Scotland down through England and into Europe, creating a ribbon or river of light; bonfires being lit throughout the land.

Humanly speaking we do not deserve any mercy from God. As a nation, there are many ways in which we have turned our back on God. We have become a laughing stock in the eyes of some other countries. Our reputation has declined in many areas of our once-proud national way of life. In recent years we have become known for our industrial strikes, for football hooliganism, for child abuse, for our divisions (between north and south, between those in work and the unemployed, between black and white), for racially inspired riots in inner-city areas, for the break-up of family life—and for a weak and ineffective church.

I am glad that God doesn't act according to what we deserve, but according to his grace and mercy. That is why I believe that those visions for revival are trustworthy.

But let us not get lost in a tide of false expectations on the one hand and empty triumphalism on the other. Nor let us sit back and wait, like surfboarders, for the next big wave of God's blessing.

Let us draw near to God. Let us cry to him. Let us praise and worship him. Let us magnify him and make much of him. Let us speak often of him to one another. Let us pray and pray and pray. Let us seek the Lord!

Do you have a vision of what God can do in your land? Are you prepared to turn that vision, that dream, into reality? Will you seek God and pray and encourage others to pray with you? Will you get up early, or stay up all night if God by his Spirit urges you to do so? Are you tuned in to hear what God will say to you by his Spirit? Are you ready to be real as you respond in glad and, for you, glorious obedience?

> These things I plan won't happen right away. Slowly, steadily, surely, the time approaches when the vision will be fulfilled. If it seems slow, do not despair, for these things will surely come to pass. Just be patient! They will not be overdue a single day! (Hab 2:3, TLB).

Thus says the Lord, and may we reply:

> O Lord, now I have heard your report, and I worship you in awe for the fearful things you are going to do. In this time of our deep need, begin again to help us, as you did in years gone by. Show us your power to save us. In your wrath, remember mercy (Hab 3:2, TLB).

Notes

1. Rene Monod, *The Korean Revival* (Hodder & Stoughton, 1971).
2. Norman Grubb, *Continuous Revival* (Christian Literature Crusade, 1952), p 48.
3. Roger Mitchell, *The Kingdom Factor* (Marshall Pickering, 1986), p 160.
4. Arthur Wallis, *Rain from Heaven* (Hodder & Stoughton, 1979), pp 122–123.
5. Nick Cuthbert, *Rise Up and Build* (Kingsway, 1982), pp 117–118.

Appendix

IPAWE is the International Prayer Assembly on World Evangelism, which was held in Seoul, Korea, in 1984. It was organised by the Lausanne Movement. The following statement was signed by all the participants at that international assembly. I was not present, although invited. I support what it is saying and have felt it right to include the statement here.

God, in his calling and providence has brought us together in Seoul, Korea, from 69 nations. We have sought his face and his guidance. He impressed on us an urgency to call for an international prayer movement to accomplish spiritual awakening and world evangelisation.

World evangelisation is a sovereign work of the triune God through the ministry of Christ's church. The forces of darkness which block the spread of truth and the growth of the church cannot be displaced by human plans and efforts. Only the omnipotent and omniscient Holy Spirit, applying the fruits of the finished work of Christ through a church constantly awakened through prayer, can deliver the lost from the power of Satan (Acts

26:27–28), 'as the Lord adds daily those who are being saved' (Acts 2:47).

The awakening of the church is thus essential to the completion of world evangelisation. The renewed church in Acts 2:42–47 was strengthened by apostolic teaching, the Lord's Supper and shared fellowship. But these means of grace can only be empowered for us today through fervent and persistent prayer to the Father in the name of the crucified and risen Christ. Even after Pentecost, the apostles repeatedly turned to prayer for the church to be filled afresh with the Spirit and empowered to proclaim the gospel with boldness, despite Satanic resistance (Acts 4:23–31).

Prayer is God's appointed means whereby the Spirit's power is released in evangelism. By prayer, the Spirit both empowers our witness and opens Satan-blinded unbelievers to seek and desire the Lord Jesus Christ as Saviour. The Lord's promise that his father will answer us if we ask according to his will and in his name is our strong encouragement in believing prayer.

Before the Lord's return to judge all Satanic rebellion and to consummate his kingdom in power and glory, the gospel must and will be preached, and disciples made, among every people on earth (Matthew 24:14; 28:19–20; Mark 13:10). Explicit agreement and visible union of God's people in extraordinary prayer for the renewal of the church and world evangelisation is essential to the extension of the kingdom of Christ through the preaching of the gospel.

We rejoice that in the last few years in many parts of the world, through the work of the Holy Spirit, there has been a growing dependence on God which has led to increased unity in prayer in the body of Christ transcending denominational, national, ethnic and cultural divisions.

We confess that too often prayer is offered only for

personal, physical and financial needs rather than for spiritual needs in the church, neighbourhood and world.

We confess that frequently there is a lack of meaningful prayer by the congregation in services of the local church as well as a general lack of personal and family prayer.

We confess that there is not enough emphasis on, training for, and dependence upon prayer from the pulpits and Christian training institutions.

We confess that too often dependence on the Holy Spirit's role in prayer has been minimised and mobilisation of prayer has been without reliance upon him.

We are constrained to call the body of Christ worldwide to mobilise intercession for spiritual awakening in the church and world evangelisation. We call specifically for:

1. The formation of interdenominational prayer committees whenever possible through existing structures on city, national, regional, continental and international levels.
2. The convening of national, regional, and continental and international prayer assemblies, as soon as this can be adequately implemented, and thereafter at regular intervals.
3. The establishing of information networks through personal visitation, literature, computer linkages, audio-visual media and other means for communicating prayer needs, emergencies, methods, reports of prayer movements worldwide, and prayer ministry resources.
4. The promotion of, nurture and teaching of prayer life through seminars, workshops, literature and audio-visual facilities.
5. The encouragement of all churches, theological seminaries, Christian institutions, parachurch organ-

isations, Christian leaders and pastors to give the highest priority and strongest emphasis to prayer, both in personal and public ministry.

6. The cooperation and participation of the church worldwide in the observance of specifically designated days of prayer. (Example: Pentecost Sunday, Prayer for World Evangelisation.)

We therefore call all believers to a specific and personal commitment to become prayer warriors for spiritual awakening and world evangelisation.